Fish & Seafood

Checkerboard Cookbooks

NEW YORK

Adapted from *I Pesci*, by Luciano Imbriani, in the series "Jolly
della Buona Cucina" (Series Editor, Luigi Carnacina; Photographs
by Umberto Marzani and Sandro Pagani)

First published in USA 1982 by Checkerboard Cookbooks
Checkerboard Cookbooks is a trademark of Simon & Schuster, Inc.
Distributed by Bookthrift, New York, NY

Editorial adaptation and production by
Accolade Books, Inc., New York, NY

Editorial director: John Kremitske
Editorial consultant: Nancy Parilla Macagno
Recipe editing and adaptation: Pam Rabin, Dale McAdoo
Introduction by: Stephen Schmidt
Layout: Marcia Rizzi
Cover design: Michael Simon

Introduction

Fish—Nature's Most Abundant and Protein-Rich Food Resource

SOME GENERAL REMARKS

For some years, culinary societies, government agencies, and various commissions set up by the fishing industry have been trying to find out why so little fish is eaten in the United States—at least relative to the vast amounts of meat and poultry that are consumed. Contrary to what one might expect, these investigative bodies have not found that people dislike fish. It seems, instead, that for various reasons people distrust their ability to shop for fish and to prepare it for the table.

Perhaps the most basic problem that the fish industry has in attracting new customers is fish nomenclature. A single fish may go by several names; likewise, closely related fish may be grouped together and sold under a single name. To take a relatively common and uncomplicated case, the large group of fish that produce so-called "sole fillets" are not true sole at all (which is not an American fish), but rather various kinds of flounder. And when a shopper sets out to buy fillet of sole at a fish market, he or she will be directed to fish that may be labeled "sole," "flounder," "flatfish," "yellowtail," "dab," and so on. It doesn't make much difference which type of "sole" a shopper chooses—they are all very similar in taste and texture—but to a fish neophyte this confusing array of names is bound to be intimidating. Luckily, several initiatives are underway at present to standardize and streamline fish nomenclature, though only time will tell how well these attempts succeed.

Other frequently cited reasons for shoppers' wariness of fish are its comparatively high price and lack of easy availability in some areas. These problems, however, prove less serious than they might appear on the surface. Only a few kinds of fish (shrimp, for example) are generally as expensive per pound as good-quality beef, and most varieties of fish cost considerably less. Further, unlike meat and poultry, fish fillets and fish steaks contain very little waste, so the shopper is paying only for edible flesh. As for availability, it is true that good fresh ocean fish is hard to find in many inland regions of the country. However, fish frozen immediately after harvesting and maintained at a constant temperature of 0°F or less is likely to be virtually indistinguishable in taste and texture from fish that is freshly caught. And freshwater fish, prevalent throughout the country, makes delicious eating and may be substituted in most recipes for ocean fish.

A belief that fish is difficult to cook has also played some part in its relative unpopularity as a dietary staple. On the one hand, it is true that unless closely and carefully watched, fish is liable to be overcooked, losing its delicate flavor and turning leathery and dry. But on the other hand, as long as one avoids the overcooking pitfall, little can actually go wrong when cooking fish. A wholesome and naturally tasty food, fish practically cooks itself. It requires little seasoning and responds well to the same simple cooking techniques that are used when preparing meat and poultry: poaching, frying, baking, and broiling. Nor is there reason for trepidation when tackling more complex fish recipes, such as some included in this volume. Because fish combines well with a wide range of flavorings, it is unlikely that a recipe will be ruined if it is accidentally modified somewhat or an ingredient is substituted.

If lingering prejudice and old habits were cast aside, fish could play a significant role in alleviating the food supply problems brought about by the world's overdependence on meat as a source of protein. Whereas most meat animals must be raised on farms, fish is an abundant and, with proper controls, perpetually self-renewing food resource. Moreover, man can cultivate many species of aquatic life (oysters, shrimp, catfish, and trout, to name just a few) using but a fraction of the land space required to produce an equal amount of meat protein.

And fish is a fine food choice because it is so naturally healthful and nourishing. The flesh of fish is made up almost entirely of protein; in fact, an adult can obtain nearly all the required daily protein by eating a single eight-ounce serving of fish. Fish contains a host of valuable vitamins and minerals, including iodine, an essential mineral nutrient found in few other foods. Fish is also lower in calories than red meat and contains no saturated fats. In sum, although the old beliefs that fish is an aphrodisiac and "brain food" have yet to be proved, modern nutritional science suggests that we will reap substantial health benefits from eating good fish regularly.

BUYING AND STORING FISH

The delicate flesh of fish is highly susceptible both to enzymatic deterioration and to bacterial spoilage; thus stale fish is likely to taste "fishy" or "muddy" and be tough, dry, or fibrous in texture. The familiar advice to buy only the freshest fish is therefore well taken, but at times the tone of this advice is so dire and stern as to make some cooks give up on fish entirely, despairing of ever finding any that measures up to such high standards. In fact, thanks to today's very efficient fishing vessels (many equipped with onboard processing plants) and rapid transport, it is possible to find good fish in nearly every part of the country. You just have to search it out.

The search for fresh fish begins, of course, at the fish market itself. Fish markets differ considerably in the care they take with their product. Because enzymatic and bacterial damage are the mortal foes of good-tasting fish, a serious fish market will keep its fish very cold, preferably laying it on beds of ice. And a very serious market will go one step further and store its fish under protective covering. It is not difficult to judge the quality of a fish market: as the comedian used to say, "the nose knows." Truly fresh fish will smell only faintly briny, the bracing aroma of the sea. If a market is pervaded by a strong odor, something's fishy—in more ways than one—and the consumer is wise to shop elsewhere.

It is easiest to determine the quality of fish when the fish is bought whole, then dressed and cut into fillets or steaks by the fish dealer while the shopper looks on. A truly fresh whole fish has a distinct look: the eyes will be clear, bright, and bulging; scales will be shiny and lie flat against the body; the gills will be moist and bright red. It is not really necessary, though, for a shopper to take along to the fish market a checklist of such telltale signs of freshness, for what all this advice boils down to is that the fish should look, more or less, the way it did when swimming about in its stream, lake, or sea home. If, on the other hand, the fish looks—or smells—like a long-dead creature, it is surely stale and will prove a disappointment when cooked.

Some people avoid buying whole fish because they think they are paying, when fish is priced by the pound, for a great deal of waste: head, fins, scales, and bones. However, the price per pound of whole fish is always considerably less than the price of fish fillets or steaks; thus there is usually no actual difference in cost between whole and cut-up fish. Furthermore, the head and bones are not really waste, for they can be easily turned into a delicious fish broth or stock. (If you wish to make a large amount of broth or stock the fish seller will supply you, often free of charge, with extra heads and bones.)

How to Prepare Fish for Cooking

HOW TO CLEAN A FISH

Remove fish scales by scraping with a fish-scaler from the tail toward the head.
◁

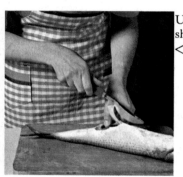

Using a sharp knife or kitchen shears, slit open the belly.
◁

Remove the entrails. If you wish to remove the head, make a circular cut with a sharp knife completely around the fish just below the gills.
◁

HOW TO CLEAN AND FILLET A SOLE OR FLOUNDER

1▷ Using a very sharp knife, cut through dark skin at the tail.

2▷ Carefully lift and pull back a little of the skin from the tail forward.

3▷ With a quick tug from tail to head, tear the skin from flesh (holding tail with a kitchen towel to keep from slipping).

In the same way, remove light skin from other side of sole. To remove head, make a diagonal slash near gills.
◁4

5▷
Using either a very sharp knife or kitchen shears, cut off spines around the edges.

Turn fish over to side formerly covered with darker skin (the top), make a shallow incision along edge, and using your finger, eviscerate the fish.
◁6

7▷
Using a knife with a flexible blade, make a cut along central spine the whole length of the fish.

With the point of the knife, lift one of the fillets, then gently separate it from spine.
◁8

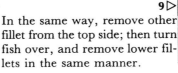

9▷
In the same way, remove other fillet from the top side; then turn fish over, and remove lower fillets in the same manner.

7

Choosing fresh fish fillets and steaks is a chancier business than choosing whole fish, but certain general guidelines can be of some help. Fish that looks moist, pinkish, and translucent is in better condition than fish that has turned milky or taken on a granular or chunky appearance. Check also to make sure the fish does not look dried out, leathery, brownish, or greasy; these are signs it has been exposed to air excessively. And when buying fish packed in cellophane-covered trays at the supermarket, avoid packages containing a great deal of liquid. Such liquid may be harmless—merely fish juice or melted ice—but it may also indicate the fish has been frozen and thawed several times, suffering substantial damage in taste and texture in the process.

Storage at Home. Once fish is brought home, it should be wrapped tightly in plastic and refrigerated at once. If the refrigerator is very cold, near the freezing point, the fish can be kept for up to two days. However, if the refrigerator temperature is 40°F or higher, as is likely the case, the fish should be served on the same day as purchased.

Provided it has not been frozen previously and thawed before being sold, fresh fish takes well to being stored in a home freezer. But the freezer must be capable of reaching a temperature of 0°F or less and maintaining that temperature constantly for as long as the fish remains frozen. Too high a temperature will allow bacteria and enzymes to continue doing their nasty work; temperature fluctuations will cause the water held in the fish to expand and contract, thus tearing the flesh and giving the fish a mushy or fibrous texture when cooked. To prepare fish for the freezer, wrap each piece tightly, first in plastic wrap and then in foil, and place pieces in a plastic bag. Squeeze the air out of the bag and secure it well. If the fish is to be kept for longer than a month, it is a good idea to wind each piece in wet cheesecloth before wrapping it in plastic wrap and foil; this impedes the penetration of air. Thaw frozen fish slowly, preferably in the refrigerator compartment to prevent damage to its texture.

Amount of Fish to Buy. When calculating how much fish you need to buy, take into account the size of the appetites of the people you are serving. Remember that fish is a light food, and thus while as little as four ounces of meat or poultry are generally sufficient for a serving, an adequate portion of fish should be closer to half a pound. When buying a whole, ungutted fish, allow almost a pound of fish per person to make up for the weight lost when the fish is dressed. If the fish has been eviscerated and trimmed of fins but left with head intact, you will need about three-quarters of a pound per person; but make suitable adjustments if the head appears either very large or very small in proportion to the body. A fish steak, which will almost always contain some bone, should weigh a half pound or more for one generous serving. But a half pound of fish fillets is a very generous portion, and you can get by with as little as 5 or 6 ounces, especially if the fillets are accompanied with a rich sauce.

VARIETIES OF FISH AND SOME SUBSTITUTIONS

When a recipe given here calls for a fish that is unavailable or much too expensive in your area, almost invariably you can prepare the recipe using some other kind of fish. The guiding principles of fish substitution are fairly simple. Fish are classified according to two main characteristics: flesh color (light-fleshed, dark-fleshed) and fat content (lean, moderately fatty, or fatty). As much as possible, the fish you choose for a substitute should match the fish called for by the recipe with respect to both of these basic qualities.

Flesh color is the more important factor. A lean fish may usually be used satisfactorily in place of a fatty fish (or vice versa), but light-fleshed fish and dark-fleshed fish are not interchangeable. The reason for this is that most light-fleshed fish are mild in taste and delicate in texture, and most recipes using light-fleshed fish will therefore call for light seasoning and a relatively brief cooking time. By contrast, dark-fleshed fish tend to be strong-flavored and firm-textured. Recipes for dark-fleshed fish will thus often include strong seasonings, heavy marinades, or piquant sauces, all of which would be likely to overwhelm the natural taste of light-fleshed fish.

About Light-Fleshed Fish. The most popular light-fleshed fish are various members of the cod family, including cod, haddock, pollack, whiting, and scrod. Except for scrod, which is actually a fish of any of these varieties weighing under three pounds, all the cod-type fish are·quite large when mature and therefore usually sold either as steaks or fillets rather than whole. Subtle-tasting, moist, and often chunky in texture, these fish may be used interchangeably in any recipe. Pollack is the firmest (and often the cheapest) of the group; whiting is the softest, sweetest, and most delicate, a fish that must be handled carefully during cooking in order not to break apart.

The bass family contains a large variety of light-fleshed fish that go by a bewildering array of names. Though each type of bass holds its special pleasures for the connoisseur, all are sweet, mild-flavored, and have delicate flesh that flakes easily. Black and white sea bass and their many close relatives will generally weigh about five pounds, a convenient size for baking or poaching whole. Striped bass and grouper generally are larger fish that are usually cut up in steaks or fillets, though both are also caught in sizes small enough to be cooked whole. Freshwater bass, ranging from one to ten pounds, are softer-textured and milder in taste than bass fished from the sea, but they may be substituted successfully in any sea bass recipe. If no bass of any sort is available at your market, you may substitute either red snapper or sea trout (weakfish), both of which will produce similar results to bass in a recipe.

Then there are the flatfish: flounder, so-called "sole," and all the many fish containing the words "flounder" or "sole" in their name. Once cooked, these fish are very difficult to tell apart in taste and texture, and all

can be used interchangeably. If you are unable to find any kind of flatfish at your market, you may use ocean perch fillets, although this fish is even more subtly flavored than the various flatfish and does not take well to rich sauces.

Mullet, red snapper, porgy, and pompano are fish that are commonly served whole, one per serving. These fish are sweet and nutlike in flavor and have soft, delicate flesh. Though each of these fish has its own following—some gourmets, for example, think pompano is the most delicious fish caught in American waters—they all take well to the same basic cooking techniques.

About Dark-Fleshed Fish. Dark-fleshed fish are more distinctive in flavor than are light-fleshed fish; thus it is more difficult to substitute one dark fish for another. Nonetheless, if you heed your culinary intuitions and make a few best-guess adjustments in a recipe, you are just as likely to produce a fine dish with a substituted fish. You may even find that the recipe you invent using a substitute fish is more to your taste than the original.

Swordfish is the American steak fish par excellence, but it is expensive and relatively scarce. However, shark, a fish becoming more readily available in fish markets, is a fine replacement for swordfish. Only the most sophisticated fish eaters will be able to tell the difference. Tuna may also be substituted for swordfish. If you find the taste of tuna too fishy, you might try marinating it in a mixture of equal parts of water, lemon juice, and olive oil before cooking.

Surprisingly, certain entirely unrelated dark-fleshed fish respond well to many of the same cooking techniques. Take bluefish and mackerel, for instance. While mackerel is stronger-tasting than bluefish, when used in recipes including other full-flavored ingredients, these two fatty, firm-fleshed fish are hard to tell apart. Likewise, trout and salmon, though they do not look anything like each other, are similar enough in taste and texture to be interchangeable in recipes involving poaching, braising, and baking. You do have to adjust cooking times to allow for the appreciable difference in size between these two fish. Lastly, though eel is eel (a very distinctive fish, to say the least), you can very likely adapt any eel recipe you fancy for carp. Carp, a freshwater fish, is softer and more gelatinous than eel, but both fish have a rich, mellow flavor that makes them ideal for sweet-and-sour sauces and for sauces having strong doses of onion or garlic.

Finally, a few words about squid, a marine creature much loved by all Mediterranean cultures but largely ignored in the United States, at least until recently. Actually, squid is not a fish at all, but it is properly mentioned in the same context as dark-fleshed fish because, like them, it is very distinctive in taste and texture. The only possible substitute for squid is octopus, which is all but unobtainable in the United States; fortunately, frozen squid is available almost everywhere. The important thing to remember when preparing squid is being careful not to overcook it. Squid is done as soon as it loses its transparent look and becomes white and firm. If cooked beyond this point, it will become rubbery and very hard to chew.

About Shellfish. Shellfish divide into two large categories: crustaceans (lobster, crab, shrimp) and bivalves (clams, mussels, oysters). Most recipes developed for one kind of crustacean are equally good when made with another, and the same holds true for recipes using clams, mussels, or oysters. Naturally, some common-sense adjustments will often be necessary when making a substitution, but all shellfish are so tasty in themselves it is rather hard to ruin a shellfish dish—unless you overcook it, the cardinal sin of shellfish cuisine.

Some cooks or hosts despair at the thought of having to pry open live oysters, but these well-protected creatures are easier to get at than might be supposed. The easiest method is to pop them into a very hot oven (500°F) for a minute or two, until they expire and let loose their grasp. Oysters may also be tackled successfully with an ordinary bottle opener. Lay the oysters on a flat surface, their protruding sides down, and poke the opener, curved side down, between the shell halves *at the hinge.* (You may have to prod a bit to find a spot where you can insert the opener.) Press down on the opener until you feel the hinge give. Then, using a paring knife, scrape along the inside of the flat shell until you sever the muscle holding the shell halves together.

PREPARING FISH FOR COOKING

Cleaning a fresh fish you have caught or have been given by fisherman friends is neither a difficult nor a terribly unpleasant task; the photo sequence in the Introduction shows how it is done, step by step. If your fish is store-bought, it will have been cleaned at the fish seller's and made ready for cooking, but you should nonetheless follow a few simple procedures before proceeding with your recipe.

If the fish is whole, the first thing to do—if your fish dealer has not done it already—is to cut away the large fanlike fin on the top side of the fish (the dorsal fin) and pull out the bones by which it is attached to the skeletal structure. Simply make an incision on each side of the fin running the whole length of the fin; then probe into the flesh and firmly tug the bones free in one piece. Next, run your fingers over the skin, especially the parts near the tail, head, belly, and back, to make sure there are no stray scales still attached. If you should find any scales, scrape them off with a dull, sturdy table knife, working over a sink or basin. Last, rinse the fish thoroughly inside and out, under cold running water and pat dry with paper towels. If when washing the belly cavity you discover traces of viscera or blood, rub the cavity with a cut lemon.

All you need do to prepare fish steaks and fillets for cooking is to rinse them quickly under cold running water and pat dry. If you wish, you may also remove any remaining small bones. Run your index finger against the grain of the flesh. If it catches on a bone, examine the area closely, prodding with your finger, to discern whether the bone is isolated or part of a cluster or row of other bones. Pull out the bones with your thumb and index finger; or if they are slippery or deeply buried, use kitchen

pliers or tweezers. Do not remove the segment of spinal column you will find in most fish steaks. This bone is so large that no diner is likely to swallow it by accident, and extracting the spinal remnant may cause the fish steak to fall apart during cooking.

COOKING FISH

Like all protein-rich foods, fish is very sensitive to heat, and because its flesh is lean and loosely packed, fish cooks—and overcooks—more quickly than meat or fowl does. Overcooked fish is tough, dry, and virtually flavorless, a disaster that not even the most sophisticated culinary tricks can undo. Therefore, it is necessary to watch over fish closely as it cooks and to begin testing for doneness some minutes before the recommended cooking time has elapsed. When the flesh has turned milky white all the way down to the bones and can be flaked easily with a fork, the fish is done. Fish should be brought to the table as soon as possible after cooking.

Frying and Deep Frying. With the exception of whole fish and very firm-fleshed varieties such as squid and abalone, fish that is to be fried or deep-fried is generally either covered with a coating of dry crumbs or flour or dipped in batter. The coating helps to protect the delicate flesh of the fish and to seal in moisture. The coating also absorbs a bit of the butter or oil and lends succulence to the lean flesh.

As long as you follow certain simple guidelines, pan-fried fish is nearly foolproof. First, be sure the skillet is lined with at least one-quarter inch of melted butter or oil so the fish does not stick, burn, or pick up a "scorched" taste. Second, do not crowd pieces in the pan or they will steam and turn soggy. Remember to use a fairly brisk flame so the fish will become nicely crisp, but don't set the heat so high that the crust becomes dark before the inside of the fish has cooked through. Avoid turning pieces of fish more than once, since they are liable to break apart.

Deep frying is a more involved procedure than pan frying, but once you have done it a few times, the technique will lose any of the apparent difficulty it may have seemed to hold for you. As with all other deep-fried foods, the most important determinant of quality in deep-fried fish is the temperature of the oil. If the oil is not hot enough, the crust will be grease-soaked; if too hot, the crust will burn by the time the inside of the fish has cooked through. The correct fat temperature for deep frying most fish is around 370°F. Many cooks find that a deep-frying thermometer makes things easier.

As a rule of thumb, allow 10 minutes' cooking time per inch of thickness for deep-fried fish (measured at the thickest part). However, if the fish has colored deeply and appears firm before the estimated cooking time has elapsed, you should test a piece by cutting into it. Fish that is less than half an inch at its thickest part (e.g., smelts, small shrimp, clams, oysters) cooks faster than thick fish does. Fried shrimp, for example, may be done in just 2 or 3 minutes.

Poaching. Poaching is a particularly good cooking technique for fish because it helps keep the flesh moist. Fish steaks and thick fillets require no special preparation prior to poaching, but thin fillets are often rolled or folded, sometimes around a stuffing, so they will not break apart. Whole fish should always be wrapped in several layers of cheesecloth, which is knotted at the head and tail to provide handles for removing the fish from the pot. It is convenient to use the long, narrow fish poacher when preparing a whole poached fish, but a poultry roaster will work just as well, provided it is long enough to hold the fish without bending. If you use a cooking container other than a fish poacher, you will probably have to prepare extra court-bouillon in order to fill the pot sufficiently to cover the fish.

There are two important things to remember when poaching fish. First, the poaching liquid should be well flavored, or else the taste may leach out of the fish into the broth. Therefore, do not skimp on wine, seasonings, or other ingredients called for in a recipe for court-bouillon. Second, fish must be poached over a very gentle flame. If it simmers, the poaching liquid is too hot. Rather, to borrow a French expression, the broth should merely "shudder," with

its surface nearly undisturbed except for an occasional breaking of large, lazy bubbles. If the poaching liquid is too hot, the fish may lose its savor and become dry or coarse-textured. And if the poaching liquid is close to boiling, the fish may even fall apart.

Poached fish is properly cooked as soon as the flesh feels firm and springy—rather than soft and squashy—when pressed with the finger. Thin fillets may be done in as little as 3 to 4 minutes if they are cooked flat; 8 to 10 minutes, if they are folded or rolled. Fish steaks need 10 to 15 minutes, depending on thickness. A large whole fish weighing 6 or 7 pounds will require anywhere from 25 to 40 minutes, depending on skin thickness and density of the flesh.

Baking. At first glance, the dry heat of an oven would seem unsuited to fish, but recipes for baked fish are always formulated in a way that ensures the fish does not toughen or dry out. The simplest precaution consists in giving the fish a protective coat of butter or oil and then basting it frequently, either with additional butter or oil or with its own natural juices, as it cooks. A more ambitious method involves surrounding the fish with a flavorful broth and baking it in a covered pan. Finally, some recipes call for baked fish to be dredged in bread crumbs and placed on a generously oiled pan. The crumbs and oil impart a "fried" appearance and taste to the fish while also serving to protect the delicate flesh.

Unless a recipe specifies otherwise, fish should be baked in an oven set at 350°F. Generally, fish takes about 10 minutes per inch of thickness (measured at the thickest part) to bake, but firm-fleshed fish, fish baked in thick

FLESH COLOR AND FAT CONTENT OF VARIOUS FISH

Fish	Flesh Color	Fat Content
Bass	light	lean
Bluefish	dark	fatty
Carp	dark	moderately fatty
Cod	light	lean
Flounder	light	lean
Grouper	light	lean
Haddock	light	lean
Mackerel	dark	fatty
Mullet	light	fatty
Pompano	light	fatty
Porgy	light	moderately fatty
Red Snapper	light	lean
Salmon	dark	fatty
Sardines	dark	fatty
Sea Trout	light	moderately fatty
Shark	dark	lean
Skate	light	lean
Smelts	dark	fatty
Sole	light	lean
Squid	light	lean
Swordfish	dark	moderately fatty
Trout (freshwater)	dark	moderately fatty
Whiting	light	moderately fatty

or highly flavored sauces, and fish that has been stuffed will take longer. When juice begins to accumulate in the pan, the fish is close to being done. Test whether it is ready to serve by attempting to flake the flesh at the thickest part of the fish.

Broiling and Charcoal Grilling. Broiled and charcoal-grilled fish will toughen and have a bitter taste if subjected to the same degree of heat used to broil or grill meat or poultry. Thus, fish broiled in a kitchen range should be set 4 to 5 inches away from the heating element, and fish grilled over charcoal should be 3 inches or more from hot coals. Burnt fish is virtually inedible, so when broiling or grilling it you must watch the fish very closely. While it is a good idea to coat broiled or grilled fish generously with butter, oil, or marinade before cooking, do not add so much butter, oil, or marinade as to risk flaming.

Broiled fish cooks quickly. Thin fillets, which should not be turned, will be done in 2 or 3 minutes. Thick fillets, fish steaks, and whole fish, which should be turned only once, will take 5 to 8 minutes per side, depending on thickness and density of the flesh. For grilling fish, a hinged wire grill basket is a recommended convenience that will keep the fish from breaking apart while cooking or when being turned.

Sauces and Seasoned Butters

Béarnaise Sauce

Yield: about 1½ cups

2 sprigs chervil, minced (or generous pinch of dried)
2 sprigs tarragon, minced (or pinch of dried)
2 shallots, minced (or scallions)
black pepper, freshly ground
5 Tb dry white wine
5 Tb wine vinegar
3 egg yolks
¾ cup butter
salt

In a saucepan, combine chervil, tarragon (reserving a pinch each for garnish), shallots, a generous pinch of pepper, wine, and vinegar. Simmer until liquid has been reduced by two-thirds. Remove from heat, and cool to lukewarm. Beat egg yolks until thick. Add 1 tablespoon of hot water, and beat for a minute or so longer. Return sauce to low heat, and add egg yolks, beating constantly with a wire whisk. Add butter in small pieces, still whisking constantly. Season to taste with salt, and continue whisking until sauce thickens.

Strain sauce through cheesecloth or a fine sieve, and serve in a sauceboat, sprinkled with reserved minced chervil and tarragon. (Béarnaise Sauce should never be exposed to high heat and should be served at room temperature.)

Béchamel

Yield: about 1 cup

2 Tb butter
½ tsp finely minced onion
2 Tb all-purpose flour
1 cup milk
salt and pepper
pinch of nutmeg, freshly grated

In a saucepan, melt butter over medium heat. Add onion and cook until transparent. Do not allow mixture to brown. Add flour and cook, stirring until well blended.

Meanwhile, bring milk almost to a boil. Pour into the flour mixture, stirring constantly, and cook until thick and smooth. Simmer another 5 minutes and season to taste with salt, pepper, and nutmeg.

This basic, medium-thick Béchamel is an all-purpose sauce called for in many recipes. For thicker Béchamel, follow the directions above, but use 3 tablespoons of butter and 3 tablespoons of flour.

Note: A cupful of most sauces should be sufficient to accompany 4 servings of fish and shellfish dishes.

Fish and Rice Cakes (p. 26)

Cocktail Sauce

Yield: about 1 cup

¼ lb butter
2 Tb tomato purée (or catsup)
2 Tb white horseradish
lemon juice
black pepper, freshly ground (or a dash of hot
   pepper sauce)

In a small saucepan, melt butter over medium-low heat. Stir in tomato purée and horseradish. Add a few drops of lemon juice and a generous sprinkling of fresh ground pepper, blending well. (This tangy sauce goes well with various shellfish.)

Creamy Dill Sauce

Yield: about 1½ cups

1 cup sour cream (or plain yogurt)
1 Tb grated onion
1 Tb oil
2 tsp lemon juice
1 heaping Tb chopped fresh dill
salt and pepper

In a blender or food processor, combine all ingredients—including salt and pepper to taste—and blend thoroughly. (Ingredients may also be whisked vigorously by hand.) Chill the sauce well when serving with cold dishes.

Curry Sauce

Yield: about 1½ cups

¼ cup minced onion
2 Tb butter
1 Tb chopped fresh parsley
1 small stalk celery, chopped
pinch of thyme
1 bay leaf
nutmeg, freshly grated
4 Tb all-purpose flour
1 tsp curry powder
2 cups fish (or vegetable) stock
⅓ cup heavy cream (or half-and-half)
lemon juice

Sauté onion in butter until wilted. Add chopped parsley and celery, together with thyme, bay leaf, and a pinch of nutmeg. Sprinkle with flour and curry powder, then whisk until well blended. Cook until the mixture begins to brown, then very gradually stir in stock. Bring to a boil, reduce heat, and simmer for about 30 minutes.

Strain the sauce, pressing the solid residue through a sieve, and return to the pan. Bring to a simmer again, stir in heavy cream, and add lemon juice to taste.

Hollandaise

Yield: about 1 cup

3 eggs yolks
1 Tb cold water
½ cup butter, melted
½ tsp salt
white pepper
1 Tb lemon juice
dash of cayenne pepper

Place egg yolks and cold water in the top of a double boiler. Set over an inch of hot (not boiling) water in the lower part, and beat with a wire whisk until fluffy. Add butter very slowly, whisking constantly, until thickened. Add salt, white pepper to taste, lemon juice, and cayenne. If you wish to thin the sauce, whisk in a tablespoon of hot water.

Mousseline

Fold 1 part whipped cream into 2 parts of Hollandaise Sauce.

Mayonnaise

Yield: about 2 cups

3 egg yolks (at room temperature)
½ tsp salt
½ tsp dry mustard
dash of cayenne pepper
¾ cup olive oil
¾ cup vegetable oil
1 Tb lemon juice (or wine vinegar)

Beat egg yolks together with salt, mustard, and cayenne until thick and lemon-colored. Combine olive and vegetable oils, and add drop by drop to the yolk mixture, beating constantly. As mixture thickens, oil may be added a little faster. Stir in lemon juice and blend well, then chill.

Mayonnaise (Blender)

Yield: about 1¼ cups

1 egg
½ tsp dry mustard
½ tsp salt
dash of cayenne pepper
2 Tb lemon juice (or wine vinegar)
½ cup olive oil
½ cup vegetable oil

In the blender container, place the egg, mustard, salt, cayenne, and lemon juice.

Combine olive and vegetable oils, and pour ¼ cup of oil mixture into blender. Cover and turn on low speed. Uncover immediately, and pour in remaining oil in a steady stream. Blend until smooth and thickened, then chill.

Mustard Dill Sauce

Yield: about 1 cup

⅔ cup oil
2 Tb lemon juice (or dry white wine)
salt
black pepper, freshly ground
1 Tb mayonnaise
½ tsp dry mustard (or 1 tsp Dijon mustard)
1 heaping Tb chopped fresh dill (or 2 tsp dill
  weed)

Combine all ingredients, including salt and pepper to taste, in a blender or food processor, and blend thoroughly; or ingredients can be vigorously whisked by hand. (This sauce can be served chilled with cold fish or seafood dishes, or else slightly warmed over very low heat for hot dishes.)

Parslied Egg and Butter Sauce

Yield: about 1¼ cups

¼ lb butter
juice of ½ lemon
salt
2 hard-cooked eggs
1 bunch parsley, chopped fine
black pepper, freshly ground

Melt butter over medium-low heat, remove from stove, and add lemon juice and a pinch of salt. Cut eggs in small wedges while still hot, then add to sauce, together with chopped parsley and a sprinkling of fresh ground pepper. Serve hot.

Rémoulade Sauce

Yield: about 1½ cups

1 cup mayonnaise
1 Tb prepared mustard
1½ tsp minced capers
2 tsp sweet pickles, chopped
1½ tsp minced fresh parsley
1 tsp chopped fresh chervil (or pinch of dried)
1½ tsp chopped fresh tarragon (or generous pinch
  of dried)
1½ tsp anchovy paste
dash of cayenne pepper

Combine all the ingredients, and continue stirring with a wooden spoon until thoroughly blended. Let sauce stand for an hour or two before serving.

Portuguese Codfish Casserole (p. 26)

Dried Cod with Sweet Peppers (p. 25)

Swedish Egg Sauce

Yield: about 1¼ cups

¼ cup butter
1 Tb all-purpose flour
1 cup milk
2 tsp prepared mustard
salt and pepper
2 hard-cooked eggs, chopped
2 tsp minced fresh parsley

In a small saucepan, melt butter over medium heat. Add flour and cook, stirring until well blended. Gradually stir milk into flour mixture until well blended. Mix in mustard and salt and pepper to taste. Cook, stirring constantly, until thickened and bubbly. Gently blend in eggs and parsley. (Serve warm with baked or poached fish.)

Creamy Shrimp Sauce

Yield: about 1½ cups

½ lb small shrimp
1 garlic clove, mashed
3 Tb butter
salt
1 cup Béchamel Sauce (See Index)

Rinse shrimp, peel and devein, then chop fine. Sauté shrimp and garlic in butter until golden, and season with a pinch of salt. (Be careful that shrimp do not darken too much while they cook.) Discard garlic clove. Press cooked shrimp though a sieve or food mill to obtain a fine-grained purée. Blend thoroughly with Béchamel Sauce.

Tartar Sauce

Yield: about 1 cup

3 hard-cooked eggs
about ½ cup oil
1 Tb wine vinegar
1 Tb minced sweet pickles
1 Tb chopped capers
1 Tb minced fresh parsley
salt and pepper

Mash egg yolks in a mixing bowl, and add oil slowly, alternating with drops of vinegar and whisking constantly. When sauce has thickened to mayonnaise consistency, add pickles, capers, and parsley. Season to taste with salt and pepper. (Optional variation: Press egg whites through a sieve, and add to sauce.)

Quick Tartar Sauce

Yield: about 1¼ cups

1 cup mayonnaise
1 Tb wine vinegar
2 Tb minced fresh parsley
1 tsp mustard
1 Tb sweet green pickle relish

Combine all ingredients in a mixing bowl or blender, and blend thoroughly.

Curry Butter

Yield: about 1 cup

¾ cup butter, softened
½ tsp curry powder
black or white pepper, freshly ground

Cream the butter until light and fluffy. Add curry powder and fresh ground pepper, blending well. (All mixing may be done either by hand or with a food processor.) Store tightly covered in refrigerator.

Maître d'Hôtel Butter

Yield: about 1 cup

¾ cup butter, softened
juice of ½ lemon
3 Tb minced fresh parsley
salt
black pepper, freshly ground

Cream the butter, and blend in all the other ingredients. Beat until mixture is light and fluffy. (All mixing may be done either by hand or with a food processor.) Store tightly covered in refrigerator; apportioning the seasoned butter among individual small ramekins, covered with foil or plastic wrap, is a convenient way of storing it.

Mixed Herb Butter

Yield: about 1 cup

¾ cup butter, softened
2 Tb lemon juice
¼ cup fresh minced herbs (e.g., tarragon, chives,
   parsley, or a combination)
salt
black pepper, freshly ground

Cream the butter until light and fluffy. Beat in lemon juice and herbs; season to taste with salt and fresh ground pepper. Blend thoroughly. (All mixing may be done either by hand or with a food processor.) Store tightly covered in refrigerator.

Saltwater Fish

Fried Anchovies with Tomato Sauce

Yield: 4 servings

2 lb fresh anchovies (or other small whole fish,
  e.g., smelts, sardines)
all-purpose flour for dredging
oil
salt
1–2 lemons, quartered
fresh parsley sprigs
1–2 cups tomato sauce, preferably homemade

Clean fish, slit open, and rinse under cold running water. Dry thoroughly, and dredge in flour. Fry fish a few at a time in enough hot oil to come about ¼ inch up the sides of the pan. When fish are crisp and golden brown on both sides, drain on paper towels and season lightly with salt. Set on a serving platter, and garnish with lemon wedges and parsley springs. Accompany with tomato sauce served in a sauceboat.

Bluefish Baked in White Wine

Yield: 4 servings

1 bluefish (about 2½–3 lb; or other moderately
  fatty fish, e.g., sea bass, sea trout)
1 small onion, sliced
2 Tb oil
1½ cups dry white wine
1 sprig fresh rosemary, crushed (or ⅓ tsp dried)
1 garlic clove, minced
salt and pepper
2–3 Tb butter
1 lemon, sliced
fresh parsley sprigs

Preheat oven to 350°. Clean fish, rinse well in cold running water, pat dry, and place in a buttered baking dish. Cover with onion slices, and moisten with oil and a few tablespoons of wine. Sprinkle with rosemary, garlic, salt, and pepper. Dot fish with butter, and bake in preheated oven until fish becomes slightly golden. Then turn fish, and baste with a little more wine. When fish is tender but still firm, turn very carefully, and baste with remaining wine. Continue cooking, basting occasionally, until fish flakes easily.

Set fish on a platter, pour cooking juices over it, and garnish with lemon slices and parsley sprigs to serve.

Salt Herring North Italian Style (p. 33)

Baked Bluefish with Zucchini

Yield: 4 servings

1 bluefish (or other moderately fatty fish;
  2½–3 lb)
salt and pepper
2 Tb butter, softened
1 lb zucchini, sliced thin
½ cup oil
¼ cup chopped fresh parsley (or dill)

Preheat oven to 350°. Clean fish, rinse well under cold running water, and dry thoroughly. Place fish in a well-oiled baking dish, season lightly with salt and pepper, and brush generously with softened butter. Arrange sliced zucchini around fish; sprinkle with salt and pepper, and dribble oil over them. Bake in preheated oven for about 30 to 35 minutes, or until fish flakes easily, stirring zucchini gently and basting with pan juices from time to time. Garnish with chopped parsley, and serve piping hot.

Chilled Herbed Fish with Saffron

Yield: 4 servings

2 lb small, fatty fish (e.g., porgy, mullet)
¼ cup oil
1 garlic clove, mashed slightly
5–6 peppercorns, bruised
1 tsp fennel seeds
½ tsp coriander seeds
bouquet garni (thyme, bay leaf, parsley)
8-oz can peeled tomatoes, chopped
salt
saffron
about ½ cup dry white wine
2 lemons, sliced

Clean fish, rinse well in cold running water, and pat dry. Put fish in a large skillet with a tight-fitting cover. Pour oil over them, and add garlic, peppercorns, fennel and coriander seeds, bouquet garni, tomatoes, a pinch of salt, and a pinch of saffron dissolved in 2 tablespoons of water. Add just enough white wine to cover. Set a sheet of oiled parchment paper or aluminum foil over the skillet, and cover with the lid. Simmer over very low heat for about 15 minutes, or until fish flakes easily. Cool fish in its cooking juices, drain, and serve chilled, garnished with lemon slices.

Baked Codfish

Yield: 4 servings

2 lb cod fillets or steaks (or scrod or haddock)
salt
juice of 1 lemon
1 onion, chopped
2 Tb butter
2 Tb oil
½ cup dry white wine
1 Tb capers
2 Tb tomato purée (or catsup)
2 eggs
3 Tb grated Parmesan cheese

Rinse fish well in cold running water, pat dry, and sprinkle with a little salt and lemon juice. Heat butter and oil in a large skillet, and sauté onion until transparent. Add cod to pan, and continue to sauté over medium heat, basting occasionally with wine. Stir in capers and tomato purée, and simmer gently until fish is tender but still firm.

Preheat oven to 425°. With a slotted spoon, transfer fish to a baking dish, then pour cooking liquid over it. Beat eggs with a pinch of salt, and pour over fish. Sprinkle generously with grated Parmesan. Bake in preheated oven for just a few minutes to set the eggs and lightly brown the cheese topping.

Dried Cod with Sweet Peppers

Yield: 4 servings

2 lb dried salt cod
3 sweet green peppers
1-lb can peeled tomatoes, chopped
3 onions, chopped
1 garlic clove, chopped
3 Tb oil
salt and pepper
oregano
hot pepper flakes

Soak dried salt cod in cold water—for 8 to 10 hours if fish is somewhat flexible, for up to 24 hours if fish is very stiff and heavily salted. Change the soaking water every 6 to 8 hours. Rinse cod under cold running water, place in a saucepan of boiling water and simmer gently for about 5 minutes. Drain, let cool slightly, discard skin, and remove bones. Cut fish in 2-inch chunks.

Set 2 sweet peppers on baking sheet, and bake in a preheated (400°) oven, turning frequently, for 15 to 20 minutes, or until skin begins to blister. Peel charred skin under cold running water, discard seeds and membrane, and cut peppers in 2-inch chunks. Combine tomatoes, onions, garlic, and oil in a deep saucepan and simmer over medium heat for 10 minutes. Season lightly with salt, pepper, and a dash of oregano and hot pepper flakes, then simmer until sauce is slightly thickened. Add pepper chunks and cod to sauce, and simmer gently for 15 minutes, or until fish and peppers are tender.

Rinse, core and seed, and dry remaining sweet pepper, and chop very fine. Add to the pan just before removing from heat. With a slotted spoon, transfer fish and peppers to a deep serving platter. Pour sauce over, and serve piping hot.

Dried Cod in Tomato Sauce

Yield: 4 servings

2 lb dried salt cod
oil
1 small onion, chopped
1 garlic clove, chopped
rosemary
1 bay leaf, crushed
2 Tb tomato paste (or ½ cup tomato purée)
1½-lb can peeled tomatoes, chopped
salt and pepper
all-purpose flour for dredging
¼ cup chopped fresh parsley

Soak and prepare dried cod according to instructions given in the preceding recipe, then bone and cut in 2-inch chunks.

Heat 2 tablespoons of oil in a saucepan, and sauté a mixture of half the chopped onion and garlic, a pinch of rosemary, crushed bay leaf, tomato paste, and chopped tomatoes. Season to taste with salt and pepper, and bring to a boil. Simmer gently over medium heat for 20 minutes. While sauce is simmering, heat enough oil to come about ¼ inch up the sides of a large skillet. Dredge cod in flour, and place in the skillet. Add remaining chopped onion and garlic, and sauté over medium heat until cod is tender, or about 5 minutes on each side. Remove cod and sautéed onions to a serving platter and keep warm. Pour tomato sauce over cod, and garnish with chopped parsley to serve.

Portuguese Codfish Casserole

Yield: 4 servings

2 lb dried salt cod
4 Idaho potatoes
4 hard-cooked eggs
⅔ cup oil
1-2 small onions, sliced
1 garlic clove, chopped
salt and pepper
10-12 black olives, sliced in half
¼ cup chopped fresh parsley

Soak and prepare dried cod according to instructions given for Dried Cod with Sweet Peppers (see Index).

Cut fish in 2-inch chunks. Boil potatoes in the jackets, and drain while still a bit underdone. Cool slightly, peel, and cut in ¼-inch slices. Peel hard-cooked eggs under cold running water and slice.

Preheat oven to 400°. Heat half the oil in a saucepan, and sauté onion slices and chopped garlic until transparent and just golden, stirring well. Grease a baking dish with a little oil; lay down first a layer of potato slices, next a layer of codfish, then one of sliced egg. Sprinkle on some sautéed onion and garlic, and continue layering until all ingredients are used up, topping off with a layer of potato slices. Garnish with ripe olive halves, dribble on the remaining oil, and bake in preheated oven for about 20 minutes. Remove from oven, and garnish with chopped parsley to serve. (In Portugal, where this is a favorite dish, it is usually served at table with oil, vinegar, and fresh ground pepper, so that guests may season their own portions to individual taste.)

Fish and Rice Cakes

Yield: 4 servings

½ lb fish fillets, poached
3 cups boiled rice
1 egg, lightly beaten
1 Tb all-purpose flour
1 Tb minced fresh parsley
grated lemon peel
bread crumbs
oil for deep frying

Flake cooked fish into a mixing bowl with a fork. Add rice, egg, flour, minced parsley and a little grated lemon peel, blending thoroughly. Form little balls from this mixture, flatten them slightly, and dredge in bread crumbs. Deep-fry in plenty of very hot oil. When fish cakes are golden brown, remove with a slotted spoon and drain on paper towels. (These simple fish cakes make an excellent light meal with a steamed green vegetable or a green salad with vinaigrette dressing.)

Porgy Baked in Parchment (p. 36)

Porgy with Mushroom Stuffing (p. 36)

Fish Fillets in Anchovy Sauce

Yield: 4 servings

2–2½ lb fish fillets
8 Tb butter
4–6 anchovy fillets, minced
3 Tb capers, minced
2 Tb oil
salt and pepper
all-purpose flour for dredging
2–3 Tb chopped fresh parsley
2 lemons, sliced

Melt 6 tablespoons of butter in a small skillet, and sauté anchovies and capers over medium heat, stirring constantly, for about 5 minutes. Melt remaining 2 tablespoons of butter with oil in a large skillet. Season fish fillets with salt and pepper, and dredge lightly in flour. Fry in butter and oil for 3 or 4 minutes on each side, or until fish flakes easily. Set fillets on a serving platter, and pour ribbons of anchovy sauce over them. Sprinkle with chopped parsley and garnish with lemon slices to serve.

Baked Fillets with Asparagus

Yield: 4 servings

2 lb fish fillets (lean or moderately fatty fish, e.g., flounder, whiting)
salt and pepper
all-purpose flour for dredging
8 Tb butter
juice of 1 lemon
2 Tb chopped fresh parsley
4 Tb grated Parmesan cheese
¾ lb asparagus tips, cooked

Rinse fish well in cold running water, and pat dry. Sprinkle with salt and pepper, and dredge lightly in flour. Heat 4 tablespoons of butter in a skillet over medium heat, and sauté fillets for a few minutes on each side, or until light golden brown. Arrange fillets in a single layer in a buttered baking dish. Stir lemon juice and chopped parsley into the pan juices in skillet, and pour mixture over fish. Sprinkle with 2 tablespoons of grated Parmesan, and dot with 2 tablespoons of butter.

Preheat oven to 425°. Heat remaining 2 tablespoons of butter in another skillet, and sauté asparagus tips just long enough to coat with butter and warm through. Arrange asparagus around fish in baking dish, sprinkle with remaining grated Parmesan, and bake in preheated oven long enough to brown cheese topping lightly. Serve piping hot.

Baked Mushroom-Flavored Fish Fillets

Yield: 4 servings

2–2½ lb fish fillets
¼ lb fresh mushrooms, sliced thin
6 Tb butter
salt and pepper
½ cup dry white wine
2 scallions, chopped (including green tops)
2 heaping Tb bread crumbs
2 Tb chopped fresh parsley

Rinse fish fillets and pat dry thoroughly. Melt 2 tablespoons of butter in a skillet, and sauté sliced mushrooms for 2 or 3 minutes. Season lightly with salt and pepper, and stir 2 tablespoons of wine into the pan. Finish cooking, stirring occasionally, for about 5 minutes, or until mushrooms are tender. Drain, reserving pan juices, and keep warm.

Preheat oven to 425°. In a buttered baking dish, spread a layer of chopped scallions, and then set fish fillets on top. Pour remaining wine and reserved mushroom juices over the fish, sprinkle with salt and pepper, and

▷

dot with 2 tablespoons of butter. Bake in preheated oven, basting occasionally, for about 15 minutes, or until fish flakes easily. Remove fillets, and reduce cooking juices over high heat. Return fish to pan, sprinkle generously with bread crumbs, dot with remaining 2 tablespoons of butter, and brown quickly under the broiler. Garnish with chopped parsley, and serve accompanied with reserved mushrooms.

Hearty Fish Fry

Yield: 4 servings

¾ lb baby squid
¾ lb small shrimp, shelled and deveined
12–16 clams, shucked
4 small sole
1 lb small whole fish (e.g., fresh anchovies, sardines, smelts)
all-purpose flour for dredging
oil for deep frying
salt
1 lemon

Clean baby squid, removing inner parts and eyes. Rinse squid and shrimp well in cold water, and pat dry. Dredge squid, shrimp, and shucked clams in flour. Clean the fish, and rinse thoroughly in cold running water; pat dry, and dredge lightly in flour.

In the following order, deep-fry fish in oil preheated to 350°: first the sole, then the small fish, and finally the squid, shrimp, and clams. When crisp and golden brown, drain on paper towels and sprinkle lightly with salt. Arrange on a warmed platter, and serve hot garnished with lemon slices or wedges.

Flounder Fillet in Mushroom Cream

Yield: 4 servings

2 lb flounder fillets (or sole)
½ lb fresh mushrooms, sliced
1 small onion, chopped
salt and pepper
1 cup dry white wine
1 cup heavy cream
2 Tb butter, softened
1 Tb chopped fresh parsley
1 Tb chopped chives

Preheat oven to 425°. Rinse fish well in cold running water, and pat dry. Combine sliced mushrooms and chopped onion, and spread in an even layer in a buttered baking dish. Arrange fillets over vegetables, sprinkle lightly with salt and pepper, and add wine. Cover baking dish with aluminum foil, and bake in preheated oven for about 15 minutes, or until fish flakes easily. Transfer fish to a serving platter, and keep warm.

Pour vegetables and cooking juices into a saucepan, and reduce liquid over high heat by about half. Add cream, lower heat, and simmer, stirring constantly, until sauce thickens. Remove from heat, blend in softened butter, and pour sauce over fillets. Garnish with chopped parsley and chives, and serve immediately.

Shrimp-Stuffed Flounder

Yield: 4 servings

1 flounder (about 2½–3 lb)
¼ lb shrimp
¼ cup chopped fresh parsley
1 garlic clove, minced
2 heaping Tb bread crumbs
salt and pepper
juice of 1 lemon
oil
tarragon (or thyme)
1 lemon, cut in wedges

Slit open and clean fish, rinse well in cold running water, and pat dry. Blanch shrimp for a minute or two, then shell, devein, and chop coarse. Combine chopped parsley, garlic, bread crumbs, chopped shrimp, a pinch of salt and pepper, and half the lemon juice. Open up fish and fill with stuffing, then press closed firmly.

Transfer flounder carefully to a platter; pour marinade consisting of oil, lemon juice, a pinch of tarragon, salt, and pepper over fish, and set aside to marinate for at least 1 hour. Drain and cook on a hot grill for about 15 to 20 minutes, basting occasionally with marinade. Garnish with lemon wedges to serve.

Braised Grouper Steaks with Tomato Sauce

Yield: 4 servings

2½–3 lb grouper steaks (or other lean fish steaks, e.g., cod, halibut, tilefish)
5 Tb butter
1 carrot, sliced thin
1 stalk celery, sliced thin
¼ cup mixed chopped herbs (e.g., thyme, parsley, bay leaf, basil, tarragon)
1½ cups dry white wine
1½ cups peeled tomatoes
¼ cup clam broth (or vegetable stock)
salt and pepper
1 tsp all-purpose flour
fresh parsley sprigs (optional)

Rinse fish steaks well under cold running water, and dry thoroughly. In a saucepan large enough to hold fish in a single layer, melt 3 tablespoons of butter and sauté carrot, celery, and herbs for 5 minutes. Arrange fish steaks atop vegetables, add white wine, and cover with a sheet of buttered parchment paper cut to the size of the pan.* Then cover with saucepan lid, and simmer over medium heat until cooking liquids are reduced by about one-half. Turn fish carefully at least once during cooking.

Pass peeled tomatoes through a food mill or sieve. Add tomatoes and broth to the pan, season to taste with salt and pepper, and cook until fish flakes easily. Set fish on a serving platter, and keep warm. Strain the sauce through a sieve, and put in a saucepan over medium heat. Combine flour with remaining 2 tablespoons of butter, and stir into sauce to thicken slightly. Pour sauce over fish, and serve immediately. You may garnish with parsley sprigs or chopped fresh parsley.

*Heavy Kraft wrapping paper or ordinary brown bag paper can be substituted for parchment.

Sea Bass with Fennel Flambé (p. 38)

Fillet of Sole with Anchovy Butter (p. 42)

Halibut au Gratin

Yield: 4 servings

4 halibut steaks (about ½ – ¾ lb each)
4 Tb butter
1 Tb all-purpose flour
1½ cups milk, heated
salt and pepper
1 egg
2 Tb grated Parmesan cheese
strip of lemon peel
2 Tb bread crumbs

Rinse fish steaks well in cold running water, and pat dry. Melt 2 tablespoons of butter, and blend in flour thoroughly until smooth. Gradually add hot milk, stirring constantly; season lightly with salt and pepper, and cook until smooth and somewhat thickened. Remove from heat, blend in egg and 1 tablespoon of grated Parmesan, and set aside to cool.

Preheat oven to 400°. Place fish steaks in a skillet or saucepan large enough to hold them in a single layer. Add water to cover, a pinch of salt, and strip of lemon peel. Bring to a boil, lower heat, and simmer gently for about 20 minutes, or until fish is tender but still firm. Drain fish steaks, skin them, and remove any bones. Butter a baking dish; arrange fish steaks in a single layer. Cover with the reserved sauce, sprinkle with mixture of bread crumbs and 1 tablespoon of grated cheese, dot with remaining 2 tablespoons of butter, and bake in preheated oven for about 10 minutes, or until topping is lightly browned and fish flakes easily.

Fresh Herring with Butter and Parsley

Yield: 4 servings

4 fresh herring (about ½ – ¾ lb each)
all-purpose flour for dredging
7 Tb butter
salt and pepper
juice of 1 lemon
¼ cup chopped fresh parsley
1 lemon, sliced (optional)
1 small onion, sliced (optional)

Clean herring, rinse well under cold running water, dry thoroughly, and dredge in flour. Melt 4 tablespoons of butter in a skillet, and sauté herring over medium heat. Season to taste with salt and pepper.

Remove skillet from heat, drain fish, and set on a warmed serving platter. Sprinkle with lemon juice and chopped parsley. Put pan with cooking juices back over the heat; add remaining 3 tablespoons of butter, simmer for a few minutes, stirring with a wooden spoon, and pour sauce over herring. Garnish with lemon slices or onion rings, if desired.

Salt Herring North Italian Style

Yield: 4 servings

4 salt herring
2 garlic cloves, sliced thin
⅓ cup olive oil
juice of 1 lemon
black pepper, freshly ground

Clean and rinse herring, remove heads, and place fish in a saucepan. Cover with cold water, bring to a boil, and simmer for a few minutes. Discard cooking water, cover fish again with cold water, and once more bring to a boil. Drain and transfer to a serving platter; garnish with slices of garlic. Combine oil, lemon juice, and a generous sprinkling of fresh ground pepper, blending well. Pour dressing over herring to serve.

Aromatic Baked Mackerel

Yield: 4 servings

1 mackerel (about 2½–3 lb; or other moderately fatty fish)
2 garlic cloves, sliced thin
1 sprig fresh rosemary, crushed (or ⅓ tsp dried)
2 Tb white wine vinegar
salt and pepper
4–5 bay leaves
1 cup red wine

Preheat oven to 375°. Clean fish thoroughly, rinse well in cold running water, and pat dry. Cut several diagonal slashes in the sides of the fish, and stud with garlic slices and bits of rosemary. Place in an oiled baking dish, sprinkle with vinegar and salt and pepper to taste, and set bay leaves on top. Bake in preheated oven for 10 minutes. Add red wine, and continue baking until wine evaporates and fish flakes easily.

Mackerel in Tomato Sauce

Yield: 4 servings

4 mackerel fillets (about ½ lb each; or bluefish)
all-purpose flour for dredging
5 Tb oil
1 small onion, chopped
10–12 pitted black olives, chopped
1-lb can peeled tomatoes, chopped
oregano
salt and pepper
¼ cup chopped fresh parsley

Rinse fillets well in cold running water, and pat dry. Dredge lightly in flour, and fry in 3 tablespoons of oil for a few minutes on each side. In a saucepan, heat 2 tablespoons of oil, and sauté chopped onion, tomatoes, and a pinch of oregano, salt, and pepper. Simmer sauce for a few minutes, stirring occasionally.

Preheat oven to 350°. Arrange fish in a single layer in an oiled baking dish. Pour in tomato sauce, sprinkle with chopped parsley, and bake in preheated oven for about 15 minutes. To serve, fish may be garnished with parsley sprigs, tomato slices, and a few whole black olives.

Sautéed Mullet with Mushroom Sauce

Yield: 4 servings

1 mullet (or other moderately fatty fish; 2½–3 lb)
4 Tb butter
1 thick slice bacon, diced
1 lb fresh mushrooms, sliced thin
about ⅓ cup fish (or vegetable) stock
salt and pepper
3 Tb oil
1 cup dry white wine
juice of ½ lemon

Melt 2 tablespoons of butter, and sauté diced bacon over medium-low heat until beginning to brown. Raise heat to medium, add sliced mushrooms, and sauté for about 5 minutes, basting occasionally with just enough stock (or hot water) to keep mushrooms moist. Sprinkle with salt and pepper to taste and continue cooking, stirring occasionally.

Clean fish, rinse well under cold running water, and dry thoroughly. In a large skillet, heat oil and remaining 2 tablespoons of butter. Add fish to the pan, and brown quickly on both sides over medium heat. Pour in wine and lemon juice, and cook at a gentle simmer for about 20 minutes, basting with a little stock or water if needed to keep from drying out. Just before removing fish from heat, stir in mushrooms and cook for a few minutes longer. Set fish on a serving platter, and smother in sautéed mushrooms to serve.

Broiled Baby Porgies

Yield: 4 servings

4 small porgies (or other small fatty fish;
    about ¾ lb each)
½ cup oil
salt
2 garlic cloves, chopped
black pepper, freshly ground
fresh majoram sprigs, chopped (or ½ tsp dried)
wine vinegar

Clean fish, rinse thoroughly under cold running water, and drain. Cut several diagonal slashes in the sides of each fish. Combine ¼ cup of oil with a bit of chopped garlic, a generous pinch of salt, and a sprinkling of fresh ground pepper. Set fish on a large platter, and pour seasoned oil over them; turn fish several times till well coated. Set fish under the broiler (preferably in a wire grill basket), and cook for about 12 to 15 minutes, turning only once and basting occasionally with more seasoned oil.

In a cup or small bowl, blend remaining chopped garlic, marjoram, and other ¼ cup of oil, seasoning with a few drops of vinegar (according to taste) and a pinch of salt and pepper. Serve in a sauceboat as accompaniment for the fish.

Grilled Sole with Maître d'Hôtel Butter (p. 42)

Porgy Baked in Parchment

Yield: 4 servings

1 porgy (about 2½–3 lb)
butter (or oil)
5 anchovy fillets, mashed
juice of 1 lemon
2 Tb vinegar
salt and pepper
4 Tb oil
2 scallions, chopped
¼ cup chopped fresh parsley
3 bay leaves

Preheat oven to 400°. Clean fish, rinse well in cold running water, and pat dry. Rub a little butter (or oil) on a sheet of heavy parchment paper or aluminum foil, and place fish in center. Combine anchovies, lemon juice, vinegar, and a pinch of salt and pepper, blending well. Stir in oil, chopped scallions, and parsley, and mix well. Spread anchovy mixture over fish, garnish with crumbled bay leaves, and carefully secure the parchment around fish.

Set fish in a baking dish, and bake in preheated oven for about 20 minutes. Serve fish still wrapped in parchment, and open it steaming in its cooking juices at table.

Porgy with Mushroom Stuffing

Yield: 4 servings

1 porgy (about 2½–3 lb; or other moderately fatty
   fish, e.g., sea bass, sea trout)
6 Tb butter
½ cup chopped scallions, including green tops
2 cups chopped fresh mushrooms
¼ cup chopped fresh parsley
1 sprig fresh rosemary, crushed (or ½ tsp dried)
salt and pepper
about 1½ cups dry white wine
1 egg
1 cup bread crumbs
1 lb potatoes
1 bay leaf

Have spine removed from fish without detaching head and tail. Clean fish, rinse well in cold running water, and pat dry. Melt 2 tablespoons of butter, and sauté scallions for 2 minutes. Add chopped mushrooms, parsley, rosemary, and salt and pepper to taste. Continue to sauté for a few minutes, stirring with a wooden spoon, and add 1 cup of wine. Turn heat high, and cook until wine evaporates. Transfer seasoned mushrooms and pan juices to a mixing bowl, and blend in egg and bread crumbs.

Preheat oven to 350°. Stuff fish with mushroom mixture, press closed, and sew up the opening with trussing twine. Peel and slice potatoes thin. Set fish in a buttered baking dish that will accommodate fish and potatoes, arrange potato slices around it, and add salt, pepper, and bay leaf. Melt remaining 4 tablespoons of butter, and pour over fish. Bake in preheated oven for about 30 minutes, then turn fish carefully and baste with a little dry wine. Continue baking, basting occasionally with a little wine and cooking juices from the baking dish, until fish flakes easily.

Italian-Style Stuffed Porgy

Yield: 4 servings

1 porgy (about 2½–3 lb; or other moderately fatty fish, e.g., sea bass, sea trout)
1 slice swordfish (about ½ lb; or shark, halibut, or other meaty fish)
1 hard roll (or 2 thick slices day-old bread)
2–3 Tb milk
1 oz dried mushrooms
2 Tb butter
4 Tb oil
1 small onion, chopped
salt and pepper
¾ cup dry white wine
2 Tb chopped fresh parsley
1 egg
nutmeg, freshly grated
5–6 slices bacon
1 bay leaf, crumbled
1 sprig fresh thyme, chopped (or pinch of dried, crumbled)
1 lemon, cut in wedges

Have spine removed from fish without detaching head and tail. Clean fish, rinse well in cold running water, and pat dry. Soak roll in milk; soak mushrooms in lukewarm water until spongy. Heat butter and 2 tablespoons of oil, and sauté onions until transparent. Add fish slice. Drain and chop mushrooms, reserving liquid for other use, and add to the pan. Stir in salt and pepper to taste and ¼ cup dry white wine, then simmer over medium heat until wine evaporates and fish is very tender. Add chopped parsley, stir to blend well, and remove from heat. Press mixture through a food mill or sieve (or mince with a knife). Squeeze soaked roll dry, mash with a fork, and add to mixture; then blend in egg and a generous dash of freshly grated nutmeg.

Stuff fish with mixture, press closed, and sew opening with trussing twine. Season lightly with salt and fresh ground pepper, then wrap in bacon slices.

Preheat oven to 400°. Butter a baking dish, and add 2 tablespoons of oil, crumbled bay leaf, and thyme. Place fish in baking dish, and bake in preheated oven until bacon is crisply browned. Remove and discard bacon. Continue cooking fish till skin is crisp and golden, basting occasionally with remaining dry wine and pan juices. Garnish with lemon wedges to serve.

Baked Stuffed Sardines

Yield: 4 servings

2 lb fresh sardines (or smelts or other small whole fish)
10–12 pitted black olives, chopped
1 garlic clove, minced
¼ cup chopped fresh parsley
½-lb can peeled tomatoes, chopped
½ cup bread crumbs
oregano
salt and pepper
3–4 Tb oil

Clean fish, slitting them open and removing entrails and spine. Rinse well in cold running water, and pat dry. In a mixing bowl, combine olives, garlic, chopped parsley, tomatoes, bread crumbs, and a generous pinch of oregano, salt, and pepper. Blend well, and stuff fish with the mixture. Press firmly to close and, handling carefully so filling does not spill out, arrange them in a single layer in a lightly oiled baking dish.

Preheat oven to 400°. Sprinkle fish with a few tablespoons of oil and a little salt, then bake in preheated oven for about 20 minutes, or until fish flakes easily.

Fried Marinated Sardines

Yield: 4 servings

2 lb fresh sardines (or other small whole fish, e.g., fresh anchovies, smelts)
all-purpose flour for dredging
oil
salt
2 cups wine vinegar
1 small onion, chopped
2 garlic cloves
2 bay leaves
oregano
peppercorns

Clean and rinse fish under cold running water. Dry well, then dredge lightly in flour. Fry a few at a time in enough hot oil to come about ¼ inch up the sides of the pan. Drain on paper towels, season lightly with salt, and set in a large bowl. Pour vinegar and 1 cup of water into a saucepan (the liquid should be enough to cover the fish), and combine with chopped onion, garlic crushed through a press, bay leaf, pinch of oregano, and a few crushed peppercorns. Simmer over low heat for about 10 minutes, then pour warm marinade over fish. Cover and refrigerate for an entire day before serving, either chilled or brought to room temperature.

Poached Sea Bass

Yield: 4 servings

1 sea bass (or other whole lean fish; 3–4 lb)
1 carrot, quartered
1 small onion, quartered
1 stalk celery, sliced thick
fresh parsley sprigs
1 lemon, cut in half
salt
5–6 peppercorns, crushed
2 Tb oil
black pepper, freshly ground

Clean fish, rinse well under cold running water, and place in a fish poacher with water to cover. Tuck vegetables and parsley around the fish, squeeze juice from 1 lemon half over all, and drop lemon rind in the pot. Sprinkle with peppercorns and a generous pinch of salt. Bring to a boil quickly, reduce heat, and poach at a very gentle simmer for about 10 minutes.

Let fish cool in poaching liquid, then transfer to a serving platter. Combine oil, fresh ground pepper and salt to taste, and juice of remaining lemon half. Mix well and pour over fish before serving. This dish can be accompanied with seasoned mayonnaise or other sauces for poached fish (see Index).

Sea Bass with Fennel Flambé

Yield: 4 servings

1 sea bass (or other whole lean fish; 3–4 lb)
½ cup fennel seeds*
1 garlic clove, minced
salt and pepper
4–5 Tb oil
½ cup brandy, warmed

* As a flavorful substitute for fennel seeds, imported dried fennel stalks or leaves can be found in specialty food shops and in the gourmet section of some supermarkets.

Clean fish, rinse well under cold running water, and dry thoroughly. Stuff the cavity with a mixture of fennel seeds and garlic. Cut 4 or 5 diagonal slashes in the sides of the fish to prevent curling during cooking. Season to taste with salt and pepper, and moisten with 1 or 2 tablespoons of oil. Place fish in a wire grill basket, and cook on a hot grill for about 30 minutes (or broil for about 15 to 20 minutes), turning occasionally and basting with oil. When fish flakes easily, open the basket and spoon out garlic-fennel stuffing onto a metal serving platter. Set fish on bed of fennel stuffing, pour heated brandy over, and flame. Flaming with brandy will give a delicate fennel flavor to the fish.

Fillet of Sole Valle d'Aosta (p. 44)

Sea Bass with Peas and Tomato Sauce

Yield: 4 servings

1 sea bass (or other whole lean fish; about 3 lb)
¼ cup oil
¼ cup chopped fresh parsley
1 garlic clove, chopped
salt and pepper
1 cup tomato sauce, preferably homemade (or 1-lb can peeled tomatoes)
½ lb shelled fresh peas (or 10-oz pkg frozen), parboiled

Clean fish, rinse well under cold running water, and dry thoroughly. Heat oil in a deep skillet large enough to hold the entire fish. Sauté chopped parsley and garlic until garlic is pale golden. Add fish to pan, and brown well on both sides over medium heat. Sprinkle with salt and pepper to taste, then add tomato sauce and partly cooked peas. Simmer gently until peas are fully cooked and tender and the sauce has thickened. Taste for seasoning, remove from heat, and serve piping hot.

Sea Bass in Aspic

Yield: 4 servings

1 sea bass (or other whole lean fish; 2½–3 lb)
1 envelope plain gelatin
1 carrot, quartered
½ onion, chopped coarse
1 stalk celery, sliced thick
fresh parsley sprigs
1 lemon, cut in half
peppercorns
salt
1 hard-cooked egg, sliced
6–8 sweet gherkins
2 potatoes, cooked and diced
3 small carrots, cooked and diced
½ lb shelled fresh peas (or 10-oz pkg frozen), cooked
1 cup mayonnaise
2 anchovy fillets, mashed
1 Tb capers
chopped fresh parsley

Prepare gelatin according to instructions on package, and let cool to the consistency of thick syrup. Clean fish, rinse well under cold running water, and place in a fish poacher with water to cover, together with carrot, onion, celery, parsley, half the lemon (after first squeezing juice into the cooking water), several peppercorns, and a generous pinch of salt. Bring to a boil quickly, reduce heat, and poach at a very gentle simmer for about 10 minutes.

Let fish cool in poaching liquid, then transfer carefully to a chopping board. Using a small sharp knife, cut a large diamond shape in skin at center of back and lift skin off, taking care to preserve diamond outline. Garnish with egg slices and spears of sweet gherkins. Combine cooked diced potatoes and carrots, peas, mayonnaise, mashed anchovies, several chopped sweet gherkins, and capers, blending well. Spoon the mixture onto a serving platter in a uniform layer, and set the fish in the center. Cover the fish and mayonnaise-vegetable bed with a light layer of gelatin. Garnish with chopped parsley and thin slices of remaining lemon half, and refrigerate until gelatin is firmly set.

Sea Perch Gourmet Style

Yield: 4 servings

4 thick slices sea perch (about 2–2½ lb; or other
   lean fish)
salt and pepper
all-purpose flour for dredging
¼ cup oil
2 hard-cooked eggs
2 Tb chopped fresh parsley
2 heaping Tb bread crumbs
juice of ½ lemon

Rinse fish well in cold running water, and pat dry. Sprinkle with salt and pepper, and dredge lightly in flour. Heat oil in a skillet, and sauté fish quickly over high heat, browning on both sides. Lower heat, and continue cooking until fish is tender but still firm.

Preheat oven to 425°. Arrange fish slices in a single layer in buttered baking dish. Mash egg yolks, combine with parsley and bread crumbs, and sprinkle mixture over the fish. Add lemon juice to cooking juices in the skillet, and dribble over the topping. Bake in preheated oven for about 10 minutes, or until crumbs are golden brown and fish flakes easily. Garnish with a mixture of chopped egg whites and more chopped fresh parsley.

Baked Stuffed Smelts

Yield: 4 servings

2 lb fresh smelts (or other small whole fish, e.g.,
   fresh anchovies, sardines)
3 anchovy fillets
1 garlic clove
2 sprigs fresh parsley
½ cup bread crumbs
½ cup grated Parmesan (or Romano) cheese
4–5 Tb oil
pepper

Clean fish, discarding bones and heads, and slash underside. Wash thoroughly under cold running water and dry. Chop anchovy fillets together with garlic and parsley. Transfer chopped ingredients to bowl, and combine with bread crumbs, grated cheese, 2 tablespoons of oil, and pepper. Mix well, and taste for seasoning; add salt if needed.

Preheat oven to 375°. Stuff fish with the filling, and sew up opening with a strong needle and heavy white thread. Set fish in a large oiled baking dish. Dribble on a few tablespoons of oil, and bake for 15 to 20 minutes, or until fish flakes easily.

Piquant Red Snapper in Brown Butter

Yield: 4 servings

1 red snapper (or porgy or sea bass; 2½–3 lb)
salt and pepper
all-purpose flour for dredging
4 Tb butter
2 Tb oil
1 lemon, peeled and mashed to pulp
12 green olives, sliced
2 Tb capers
4 anchovy fillets, chopped
¼ cup chopped fresh parsley

Clean fish, rinse and dry thoroughly. Cut several diagonal slashes into the sides. Sprinkle lightly with salt and a little pepper, then dredge lightly in flour. In a large skillet, heat 2 tablespoons of butter and oil, and sauté fish over medium-high heat for 2 or 3 minutes. Turn carefully, reduce heat to medium, and cook until almost tender. A few minutes before removing from heat, add lemon pulp, olives, capers, anchovy, and parsley, stirring to blend well. Set fish on a heated serving platter, and pour sauce from the pan over it. Brown remaining 2 tablespoons of butter, and dribble it over the fish just before serving.

Sautéed Red Snapper with Olives

Yield: 4 servings

1 red snapper (or porgy or sea bass; 2½–3 lb)
salt
all-purpose flour for dredging
¼ cup oil
2 garlic cloves, crushed
fresh rosemary, crushed (or ½ tsp dried)
1 bay leaf, crushed
wine vinegar
16–24 black olives, pitted

Clean fish, rinse well under cold running water, and dry thoroughly. Cut two diagonal slashes into the side. Sprinkle lightly with salt and dredge in flour. Heat oil in a large deep skillet, and sauté fish over medium heat until well browned, turning it only once. Lower heat, then add crushed garlic, rosemary, and bay leaf and continue cooking, basting occasionally with a few drops of vinegar and the pan juices. About 3 minutes before removing from heat, add olives, just to warm through. Set fish on a platter, pour cooking juices over it, and surround with olives to serve.

Fillet of Sole with Anchovy Butter

Yield: 4 servings

2 lb sole fillets (or flounder)
8 Tb butter
8 anchovy fillets, minced
black pepper, freshly ground
all-purpose flour for dredging
2 eggs, lightly beaten
salt
bread crumbs for dredging
2 Tb oil
1 lemon, sliced

In a mixing bowl, cream 6 tablespoons of butter with a wooden spoon. Mash anchovies, and blend well with creamed butter. Season to taste with fresh ground black pepper. Spread anchovy butter on a piece of aluminum foil or waxed paper, roll in a sausage shape, and refrigerate.

Rinse fish in cold running water, and pat dry thoroughly. Dredge lightly in flour, dip in beaten egg seasoned with a pinch of salt, then dredge in bread crumbs. Heat remaining 2 tablespoons of butter with oil, and fry fillets for 3 or 4 minutes on each side until golden brown. Transfer to a serving platter, dot each fillet with chilled anchovy butter, and garnish with lemon slices to serve.

Grilled Sole with Maître d'Hôtel Butter

Yield: 4 servings

4 small sole (or flounder)
8 Tb butter
3 Tb chopped fresh parsley
juice of ½ lemon
black pepper, freshly ground
salt

In a mixing bowl, cream 6 tablespoons of butter with a wooden spoon. Add chopped parsley, lemon juice, and a generous pinch of fresh ground pepper, blending well. Spread mixture on aluminum foil or waxed paper, roll it, and refrigerate. Melt remaining 2 tablespoons of butter.

Clean fish, rinse well in cold running water, and pat dry. Season lightly with salt and fresh ground pepper, brush with a little melted butter, and cook on a medium-hot grill, basting occasionally with melted butter and turning them only once. When fish are golden brown and flake easily, transfer to a platter, and set 2 thin pats of chilled Maître d'Hôtel Butter on each fish.

Savory Baked Tuna Steaks (p. 49)

Grilled Lobster Flambé (p. 62)

Fillet of Sole St-Germain

Yield: 4 servings

2 lb sole fillets (or flounder)
salt
black pepper, freshly ground
6 Tb butter, melted
bread crumbs for dredging
Béarnaise Sauce (see Index)
fresh parsley sprigs
1 lemon, sliced

Rinse fish well in cold running water, and pat dry; sprinkle lightly with salt and fresh ground pepper. Dip fillets in melted butter, then dredge in bread crumbs, pressing crumbs firmly into flesh. Brush with a little melted butter, place in a grill basket, and cook on a hot grill (or under a broiler), basting occasionally with melted butter and turning grill basket to brown lightly on both sides.

Prepare Béarnaise Sauce. Set grilled fillets on a serving platter, garnished with fresh parsley sprigs and lemon slices. Accompany with the sauce in a sauceboat for individual service at table.

Fillet of Sole Valle d'Aosta

Yield: 4 servings

2 lb sole fillets (or flounder)
2 Tb butter
2 Tb all-purpose flour
2 cups milk, heated
salt and pepper
about 1 cup dry white wine
1 bay leaf
4–5 peppercorns
6 oz fontina (or Muenster) cheese, sliced

Melt butter in a saucepan, then add flour, stirring constantly until smooth and well blended. Add hot milk in a slow stream, and stir until somewhat thickened. Season to taste with salt and pepper. Reserve white sauce and keep warm.

Preheat oven to 375°. Rinse fish well in cold running water, and pat dry. Flatten fillets gently with a meat pounder or the flat side of a cleaver, and place them in a buttered baking dish in one layer. Add dry white wine to just cover, bay leaf, crushed peppercorns, and a light sprinkling of salt. Cover baking dish with aluminum foil, and bake in a preheated oven for about 10 minutes. Remove from oven and raise heat to 425°. Drain fillets, discarding liquid in pan. Return fillets to baking dish, and cover with cheese slices. Pour reserved sauce over all, and bake for about 15 to 20 minutes, or until top is lightly browned.

Stockfish Sicilian Style

Yield: 4 servings

2 lb stockfish (already soaked)*
1 Tb raisins
½ cup oil
1 small onion, chopped
1 garlic clove, mashed
½ cup dry white wine
1-lb can peeled tomatoes, chopped
salt and pepper
4 potatoes, peeled and diced
about 2 doz black olives, pitted
1 Tb pine nuts
1 Tb capers

Remove skin and bones from stockfish. Dry fish thoroughly, and cut in chunks. Soak raisins in wine. Heat oil in an ovenproof casserole, and sauté onion and whole garlic clove until garlic is dark gold in color. Discard garlic, add stockfish, and sauté until fish is well browned. Drain raisins, add wine to pan, and simmer gently until wine has evaporated.

Preheat oven to 350°. Add tomatoes to casserole, together with enough water to cover the fish, and season to taste with salt and pepper. Bring to a boil, then add potatoes, olives, pine nuts, capers, and raisins. Cover pan and bake in preheated oven for about 1 hour. Check pan from time to time to see that sauce has not thickened too much. If so, add a tablespoon or two of hot water (or fish or vegetable stock).

* Stockfish is air-dried unsalted cod, haddock, pollack, or hake. It must be soaked for at least 24 hours before cooking. Water should be changed about every 6 hours.

Stockfish with Olives and Squash

Yield: 4 servings

2 lb stockfish (already soaked)*
¼ cup oil
1 medium-size onion, chopped
4 potatoes, peeled and diced
1 Tb tomato paste
1 lb butternut squash, peeled and diced
about 3 doz black olives, pitted
paprika
salt

Remove skin and bones from stockfish. Dry fish thoroughly, and cut in chunks. Heat oil in a large saucepan with a tight-fitting lid, and sauté onions until transparent. Add potatoes and tomato paste diluted with a little water. Cook for about 5 minutes to flavor, then add enough water to cover potatoes. Reduce liquid slightly, add stockfish, squash, olives, a pinch of paprika, and salt to taste. Cover and simmer for about 1 hour without stirring, but shaking the pan gently from time to time. After it has been cooking for about 20 to 30 minutes, test for seasoning and add salt if needed.

* Stockfish is air-dried unsalted cod, haddock, pollack, or hake. It must be soaked for at least 24 hours before cooking. Water should be changed about every 6 hours.

Swordfish Casserole

Yield: 4 servings

2 lb swordfish steaks
salt and pepper
⅔ cup olive oil
2 lb potatoes, sliced thin
1 large onion, sliced thin
1 garlic clove, minced
1 Tb chopped fresh parsley
½ hot pepper, minced

Rinse fish steaks well in cold running water, and pat dry. Sprinkle with salt and pepper. Preheat oven to 375°. Rub moderately deep baking dish with olive oil, and layer bottom with half of potato and onion slices. Add the fish steaks in a single layer, and cover with remaining potatoes and onion, garlic, chopped parsley, and minced pepper. Pour on remaining oil. Bake in preheated oven for about 1 hour, or until potatoes are tender and top is golden.

Piquant Swordfish Steaks

Yield: 4 servings

4 swordfish steaks (½ – ¾ lb each; or cod or
    halibut steaks)
1-lb can peeled tomatoes
½ cup pitted green olives, chopped
1 Tb capers
3 anchovy fillets, chopped coarse
2 Tb oil
2 Tb fish (or vegetable) stock
½ cup dry white wine
¼ chopped fresh parsley
salt
black pepper, freshly ground

Press tomatoes through a food mill or sieve into a deep skillet or saucepan large enough to hold fish steaks in a single layer. Stir in olives, capers, anchovies, oil, and stock (or else equal amount of water). Bring to a boil, lower heat, and simmer for about 15 minutes, or until sauce thickens.

Rinse swordfish steaks well in cold running water, pat dry, and arrange in the pan atop sauce. Add dry wine and chopped parsley. Season to taste with salt and fresh ground pepper, and simmer over medium heat, turning steaks once, until fish is tender and flakes easily.

Breaded Fish Steaks

Yield: 4 servings

4 thick fish steaks (½ – ¾ lb each; e.g., swordfish,
    halibut, shark)
1 egg
flour for dredging
salt and pepper
bread crumbs for dredging
oil
1 lemon, cut in wedges

Rinse fish steaks well in cold running water, and pat dry. In a shallow soup plate, beat egg with a pinch each of salt and pepper. Dredge steaks lightly in flour, dip into beaten egg, then in bread crumbs, pressing crumbs firmly and evenly over the fish. In a large skillet, heat enough oil to come about ¼ inch up the sides. Fry fish steaks until golden brown on both sides and fish flakes easily with a fork. Drain on paper towels, then with a spatula transfer carefully to a platter. Garnish with lemon wedges, and serve immediately.

Poached Carp in White Wine (p. 53)

Fish Steaks in Mushroom Tomato Sauce

Yield: 4 servings

4 thick fish steaks (½ — ¾ lb each; e.g.,
   swordfish, halibut, shark)
1 small onion, sliced
oil
½ lb fresh mushrooms, sliced
1-lb can peeled tomatoes
salt and pepper
1 Tb chopped fresh basil (or 1 tsp dried)
flour for dredging
1 Tb chopped fresh parsley

Rinse fish steaks well in cold running water, and pat dry. In a saucepan, sauté sliced onion in 2 tablespoons of oil until transparent. Add sliced mushrooms, and continue to sauté for a few minutes. Press tomatoes through a food mill or sieve, and stir in with sautéed vegetables. Season lightly with salt and pepper, add basil, and simmer over low heat until sauce thickens.

In a large skillet, heat enough oil to come about ¼ inch up the sides. Dredge fish steaks lightly in flour, and fry until light golden on both sides, then put them into mushroom tomato sauce. Simmer gently in sauce for about 10 minutes, turning them carefully several times for flavoring. Taste and adjust for seasoning. Serve piping hot with a garnish of chopped fresh parsley.

Teriyaki Fish Steaks

Yield: 4 servings

4 fish steaks (fresh salmon, tuna, or halibut;
   ½ – ¾ lb each)
salt and pepper
all-purpose flour for dredging
oil
2 stalks celery, sliced
3–4 scallions (or shallots; including green tops),
   chopped
3 Tb wine vinegar
2 Tb soy sauce
½ tsp dry mustard
sugar

Rinse fish steaks well in cold running water, and pat dry. Season to taste with salt and pépper, then dredge lightly in flour. In a large skillet, heat a generous amount of oil, and sauté fish steaks until browned lightly on both sides. Add sliced celery and scallions, and continue to sauté a few minutes longer.

Meanwhile, mix vinegar and soy sauce; dissolve dry mustard and a pinch of sugar in mixture, and pour over fish in the skillet. Lower heat, and simmer gently for about 8 to 10 minutes, or until fish is tender. Turn fish steaks, and baste with sauce occasionally. Accompany with cooked white rice.

Creamed Tuna Steaks

Yield: 4 servings

4 fresh tuna steaks (½ - ¾ lb each)
salt and pepper
3 Tb butter
2 Tb oil
1 small onion, sliced thin
3 Tb chopped fresh parsley
3 Tb capers, rinsed
1 tsp grated lemon peel
⅔ cup heavy cream (or half-and-half)

Rinse fish steaks well in cold running water, and pat dry. Season lightly with salt and pepper.

In a large skillet, heat butter and oil. Sauté onion briefly, then add tuna steaks and cook over medium heat for 4 or 5 minutes on each side. Add chopped parsley, capers, grated lemon peel, and heavy cream. Simmer very gently, turning steaks several times, until sauce is slightly reduced and tuna is tender. Taste for seasoning, and adjust with salt and pepper if necessary. Transfer fish and sauce to a deep platter, and serve immediately.

Savory Baked Tuna Steaks

Yield: 4 servings

4 fresh tuna steaks (½ – ¾ lb each)
4 tsp wine vinegar
salt
black pepper, freshly ground
1 medium-size onion, chopped
¼ cup chopped fresh parsley
1 lemon, sliced
1 heaping Tb capers
4 Tb oil

Preheat oven to 375°. Rinse fish steaks well in cold running water, and pat dry. Set steaks on individual squares of oiled or buttered aluminum foil, and moisten each with a teaspoonful of vinegar. Season lightly with salt and fresh ground pepper, and sprinkle some chopped onion and parsley on each, topped with a thick slice of lemon and a few capers. Dribble a tablespoonful of oil over each seasoned steak, and close the foil packets, sealing the edges securely. Bake in preheated oven for 10 to 12 minutes. To retain flavorful steaming juices, keep foil packets closed until individually served at table.

Tuna Steaks with Bacon

Yield: 4 servings

4 fresh tuna steaks (½ – ¾ lb each)
salt
black pepper, freshly ground
all-purpose flour for dredging
oil
⅓ cup dry white wine
3–4 slices bacon, minced
1 garlic clove, chopped
1 small onion, chopped
4 anchovy fillets, chopped
¼ cup chopped fresh parsley
1-lb can peeled tomatoes

Rinse fish steaks well in cold running water, and pat dry. Season with salt and fresh ground pepper, then dredge lightly in flour. In a large skillet, heat 2 or 3 tablespoons of oil, and brown the fish steaks on both sides. Add wine, increase heat, and simmer until wine evaporates. Carefully transfer steaks to a serving platter.

In the same skillet, sauté bacon over low heat for 5 minutes. Add garlic and onion, and sauté over medium heat until onion is wilted. Stir in anchovies and half the parsley. Press tomatoes through a food mill, add to sautéed vegetable and anchovy mixture, and season with salt if necessary. Simmer tomato sauce for 15 minutes, then add tuna steaks and continue simmering very gently, turning carefully several times, until fish is tender. Before removing from heat, sprinkle with remaining chopped parsley.

Sautéed Whiting in Sage Butter

Yield: 4 servings

1 whiting (about 2½–3 lb; or other moderately
 fatty fish)
5 Tb butter
6–8 fresh sage leaves
salt
black pepper, freshly ground
1 lemon, cut in wedges

Clean fish, rinse well in cold running water, and pat dry. Melt butter, and sauté sage leaves over medium heat until they begin to darken. Add fish to pan, and sauté until light brown on both sides and fish flakes easily. Season with salt and fresh ground pepper, transfer to a platter, and pour pan juices over fish to serve, garnished with lemon wedges.

Whiting with Mushroom and Almond Sauce

Yield: 4 servings

4 whiting (about ¾ lb each)
2 Tb oil
4 Tb butter
2 small onions, chopped
¼ cup chopped fresh parsley
2 garlic cloves, minced
½ lb fresh mushrooms, sliced thin
4 medium-size ripe tomatoes, sliced thin
salt
black pepper, freshly ground
fresh parsley sprigs
1 onion, sliced
1 carrot, quartered
1 stalk celery, sliced
1 bay leaf
½ lemon
4–5 peppercorns, bruised
5 Tb all-purpose flour
2–3 Tb bread crumbs
¼ cup chopped almonds

Heat oil and 2 tablespoons of butter, and sauté chopped onions, parsley and garlic for a few minutes. Add mushrooms, tomatoes, and salt and fresh ground pepper to taste. Simmer gently for 10 to 15 minutes, or until mushrooms are tender.

Clean fish, and rinse well in cold running water. Pour 6 cups of water in a large saucepan. Add parsley sprigs, sliced onion, carrot, celery, bay leaf, lemon half, and peppercorns. Bring to a boil, and simmer rapidly for about 15 minutes. Add fish to this *court-bouillon*, return liquid to a boil, lower heat, and simmer gently for a few minutes. Transfer fish to a platter, and strain the cooking broth.

Melt remaining 2 tablespoons of butter in a small saucepan. Sprinkle in the flour, and blend well with a wooden spoon. Gradually stir in *court-bouillon*. Season to taste with salt and pepper, and simmer for 5 or 6 minutes.

Preheat oven to 425°. Pour half the mushroom and tomato mixture into a baking dish. Arrange fish in a layer on top, and cover with white sauce. Spoon remaining mushroom and tomato sauce on top. Sprinkle with bread crumbs and chopped almonds, and bake in preheated oven until sauce is bubbly and top is nicely browned.

Fried Anchovies with Tomato Sauce (p. 22)

Freshwater Fish

Piquant Pan-Fried Bass

Yield: 4 servings

4 small freshwater bass (black, striped, or rock;
*   about ¾ –1 lb each)*
bread crumbs for dredging
1 Tb chopped rosemary (or 1 tsp dried)
1 Tb celery seed
⅓ cup oil
1 medium-size onion, sliced
salt and pepper
3 Tb wine vinegar

Clean fish, rinse well in cold running water, and pat dry. Make a few slashes in the sides of each. Combine bread crumbs with rosemary and celery seed, and dredge fish in the mixture, spreading crumbs evenly and pressing them firmly into the fish.

In a large skillet, sauté breaded fish in hot oil, together with sliced onion. Season to taste with salt and pepper, turning fish carefully once, and sprinkle each side with vinegar. When fish are a rich golden brown, remove from heat, and sprinkle with another tablespoonful of vinegar before serving.

Fried Carp

Yield: 4 servings

2 lb carp fillets
salt and pepper
1 egg, lightly beaten
fine white cornmeal for dredging
oil
fresh parsley sprigs
1 lemon, quartered

Rinse fish well in cold running water,* and pat dry. Sprinkle fillets with salt and pepper, dip in beaten egg, and dredge lightly in cornmeal. Heat enough oil to come about ¼ inch up the sides of a skillet, and fry carp until golden brown on both sides. Transfer to a heated platter, and garnish with parsley sprigs and lemon wedges to serve.

* This is particularly important for strong-flavored fish such as carp.

Poached Carp in White Wine

Yield: 4 servings

1 whole carp (about 2½–3 lb)
about 1 cup dry white wine
salt and pepper
3 Tb butter
1 Tb all-purpose flour
fresh parsley sprigs
1 lemon, sliced

Clean fish thoroughly, leaving head intact, and rinse very well in cold running water.* Generously butter a fish poacher, set carp in it, and add dry white wine to cover fish about halfway. Sprinkle lightly with salt and pepper, and simmer over medium heat for about 30 minutes, or until fish flakes easily.

Drain carp, and transfer to a serving platter. Simmer poaching liquid over brisk heat to reduce a bit. Blend butter and flour, and stir into the pan. Reduce sauce further over medium heat, and pour into a sauceboat to serve with the fish. Garnish fish with parsley sprigs and lemon slices. Parslied potatoes are an excellent accompaniment for simple poached fish dishes.

* This is particularly important for strong-flavored fish such as carp.

Poached Carp with Mayonnaise

Yield: 4 servings

1 whole carp (about 2½–3 lb)
1 small onion, chopped
bay leaf
fresh parsley sprigs
⅓ cup wine vinegar
4–5 peppercorns, bruised
salt
lettuce leaves
6 Tb oil
2 Tb lemon juice (or wine vinegar)
black pepper, freshly ground
1 cup mayonnaise
6–8 anchovy fillets
2–3 Tb capers
10–12 pitted black olives
2 hard-cooked eggs, quartered

Clean fish thoroughly, leaving head intact, and rinse very well in cold running water.* Set carp in a fish poacher, and add water just to cover. Add onion, bay leaf, parsley, vinegar, peppercorns, and a pinch of salt. Bring to a boil, reduce heat, and simmer over medium heat until fish flakes easily. Let stand to cool in the poaching liquid.

Line an oval serving platter with lettuce leaves. Combine oil and lemon juice with salt and pepper to taste, blend well, and pour over lettuce. Set carp on lettuce. Spoon mayonnaise into a pastry decorating bag, and cover fish completely with ribbons of mayonnaise. Garnish with anchovy fillets, capers, olives, and wedges of hard-cooked egg.

* This is particularly important for strong-flavored fish such as carp.

Eel aux Fines Herbes

Yield: 4 servings

1 eel (about 2–2½ lb)
juice of 1 lemon
1 cup oil
2 bay leaves, crushed
¼ cup chopped fresh parsley
peppercorns
salt
6 Tb butter
1½ cups dry white wine
½ cup vinegar
1 heaping Tb mixed herbs, chopped (e.g., chervil,
    tarragon, rosemary; or 1 tsp dried mixture)
1 small onion, sliced thin
1 egg yolk

To prepare eel, use a sharp-pointed knife to make an incision around the head. Next, using a kitchen towel to get a good grip, hold the fish tightly in one hand and, with pliers, skin it with one swift tugging motion. Rinse well under cold running water. Drain eel and pat dry; cut in slices about 1½ inches thick.

Prepare a marinade with lemon juice, oil, bay leaf, chopped parsley, several crushed peppercorns, and a pinch of salt. Pour marinade over eel, and marinate for at least 2 hours, turning the slices occasionally. Drain eel and cook on a very hot grill (or under the broiler), turning often and basting with a little oil from time to time.

Melt butter in a saucepan, and stir in wine, vinegar, chopped herbs, onion, and several crushed peppercorns. Simmer to reduce by about one-third, then remove sauce from heat and let stand to cool. When sauce is tepid, strain it and blend in egg yolk, first beaten lightly together with a little water. Return to low heat, and continue stirring until sauce thickens to consistency of slightly runny mayonnaise. Arrange eel on a serving platter, and pour sauce over to serve.

Eel with Mushroom Sauce

Yield: 4 servings

1 eel (about 2–2½ lb)
2 oz dried mushrooms
1 small onion
1 small carrot
1 stalk celery
10–12 fresh basil leaves (or ½ tsp dried oregano)
1 small bunch fresh parsley
4 Tb butter
1 Tb oil
all-purpose flour for dredging
½ cup dry white wine
½-lb can peeled tomatoes
salt and pepper
fish (or vegetable) stock

Skin and clean eel as in recipe for Eel aux Fines Herbes (see Index). Rinse well and pat dry, cut in slices about 1 inch thick. Soak mushrooms in warm water until spongy.

Chop together onion, carrot, celery, basil, and parsley. Sauté chopped vegetables briefly in butter and oil. Dredge eel lightly in flour, then brown on all sides in same pan with vegetables. Pour in white wine, and simmer over low heat until wine evaporates.

Rinse mushrooms and chop. Strain peeled tomatoes, and add to the saucepan, together with mushrooms. Season to taste with salt and pepper, and finish cooking over medium-low heat, basting occasionally with a little stock (or hot water) to keep very moist.

Clams Marinara (p. 62)

Gourmet Eel

Yield: 4 servings

1 eel (about 2–2½ lb)
2 oz lard
1 cup oil
⅓ cup vinegar
1 small onion, sliced thin
1 bunch fresh parsley
salt
black pepper, freshly ground
4 Tb butter, softened
¼ cup chopped fresh parsley
1 lemon, sliced thin

Skin and clean eel as in recipe for Eel aux Fines Herbes (see Index). Rinse well and pat dry. Rub eel thoroughly with lard, then cover with marinade made of oil, vinegar, onion, parsley crushed in a mortar, and a pinch each of salt and fresh ground pepper. Marinate for several hours.

Preheat oven to 375°. Drain eel, roll in a circle, secure with a long wooden or stainless steel skewer, and set in a well-buttered baking dish. Dot with butter, and bake in preheated oven for about 30 to 40 minutes. Garnish with chopped parsley and lemon slices to serve.

Batter-Fried Lake Perch

Yield: 4 servings

4 small lake perch (about ¾–1 lb each)
salt
2 eggs, lightly beaten
bread crumbs
1 Tb chopped chervil (or 1 tsp dried)
4 Tb butter
1 lemon
fresh parsley sprigs

Clean and fillet perch; rinse well in cold running water. Skin and tenderize fish by beating gently with a broad knifeblade. Dip in lightly salted beaten egg, then in bread crumbs mixed with chervil, pressing firmly with the hands to ensure even breading.

Foam butter in a skillet, and fry perch fillets over medium heat, turning carefully twice to ensure even browning on both sides. Transfer to a platter, and garnish with lemon wedges and parsley sprigs to serve.

Baked Pike

Yield: 4 servings

1 whole pike (about 2½–3 lb)
1 thick slice bacon, diced
4 Tb butter
salt
black pepper, freshly ground
½ cup dry white wine
1 tsp Dijon mustard (or ½ tsp dry mustard)
1 Tb all-purpose flour

Preheat oven to 400°. Clean the fish, rinse well in cold running water, and pat dry. Cut tiny slits in the fish, and insert bits of bacon. Set pike in a buttered or oiled baking dish, dot with 2 tablespoons of butter, and sprinkle with salt and fresh ground pepper. Bake in preheated oven until fish is nicely browned. Baste with dry wine blended with mustard, and continue baking, basting occasionally, for about 15 minutes, or until fish flakes easily.

Transfer fish to a serving platter and keep hot. Mix remaining 2 tablespoons of butter with flour, and add pan juices. Set over low heat, and stir constantly until smoothly blended. Pour sauce over baked pike, and serve immediately.

Pike with Walnuts au Gratin

Yield: 4 servings

2–2½ lb pike steaks
1 oz dried mushrooms (about 1 cup)
salt and pepper
all-purpose flour for dredging
6 Tb butter
1 clove
1 bay leaf
1 small onion, chopped
1 stalk celery, chopped
¼ cup chopped fresh parsley
½ cup dry white wine
½ cup fish (or vegetable) stock
½ cup walnuts, chopped
2 heaping Tb grated Gruyère cheese

Soak mushrooms in warm water until spongy. Rinse fish well in cold running water, and pat dry. Season with salt and pepper, and dredge lightly in flour.

In a large skillet, heat 4 tablespoons of butter until foamy, and sauté fish steaks until light brown on both sides. Add clove, bay leaf, and chopped onion, celery, and parsley. Cook for several minutes to blend flavors, then pour in dry wine and stock. Drain and chop mushrooms, add to the pan, cover, and simmer over medium-low heat for about 15 minutes.

Preheat oven to 400°. Remove fish from skillet with a slotted spoon, and transfer to a lightly oiled baking dish. Strain cooking liquid into a saucepan, and cook over high heat until slightly thickened. Stir in chopped walnuts, and pour sauce over fish. Sprinkle with grated Gruyère, and dot with remaining 2 tablespoons of butter. Bake in preheated oven until top is well browned.

Baked Trout with Smoked Salmon Stuffing

Yield: 4 servings

1 whole brook or rainbow trout (about 3–3½ lb)
salt and pepper
about 2 cups milk
¼ lb smoked salmon, chopped
1 Tb chopped fresh dill (or 1 tsp dill weed)
¼ cup fine bread crumbs
all-purpose flour for dredging
2 eggs, lightly beaten
4–5 Tb butter
½ cup dry white wine
1 Tb lemon juice
4 slices buttered toast

Clean trout, rinse well in cold running water, and pat dry. Place fish in a deep dish, season lightly with salt and pepper, add enough milk to just cover, and set aside to soak for at least 1 hour. Combine chopped salmon, dill, and bread crumbs, mixing well. Drain and dry fish thoroughly. Stuff with salmon mixture, and close securely with trussing twine.

Preheat oven to 400°. Dredge fish lightly in flour, and dip in beaten egg. Heat butter until foaming, and sauté trout until browned lightly on both sides. Transfer fish to a buttered baking dish, and baste with a mixture of dry wine and lemon juice. Bake in preheated oven for about 25 to 30 minutes, basting occasionally. Serve piping hot, on a platter surrounded with buttered toast points.

Stuffed Trout

Yield: 4 servings

1 whole brook or rainbow trout (about 3–3½ lb)
1 chicken liver
¼ lb cooked ham (preferably smoked)
1 Tb brandy (or dry sherry)
4 Tb butter
1 small onion, chopped
1 parboiled carrot, chopped
2 Tb chopped fresh parsley
2 heaping Tb bread crumbs
1 cup dry white wine
salt

Clean trout, rinse well in cold running water, and pat dry. Cut several diagonal slashes in the sides. Chop chicken liver and ham fine, or press through a food mill. Add brandy and 2 tablespoons of butter, blend well, and stuff trout with the mixture. Sew closed with trussing twine.

Preheat oven to 350°. Melt remaining 2 tablespoons of butter in a heatproof casserole, and sauté onion and carrot until tender. Add parsley and bread crumbs, then sauté for 2 or 3 minutes longer.

Set trout in casserole with vegetables, add wine, and season to taste with salt. Cover and bake in preheated oven for about 30 minutes, or until fish flakes easily, basting occasionally with pan juices.

Grilled Brook Trout with Parslied Butter

Yield: 4 servings

4 small brook trout (about ¾–1 lb each)
1 scant cup oil
about 4 Tb lemon juice
salt
ginger root, freshly grated (or powdered ginger)
5 Tb butter, softened
3 Tb fresh chopped parsley
white pepper, freshly ground
2 lemons, sliced
fresh parsley sprigs

Clean fish, rinse well in cold running water, and pat dry. Make a few diagonal slashes in their sides, and set them on a deep plate. Combine oil, 3 tablespoons of lemon juice, a pinch of salt, and a dash of freshly grated ginger, blending well. Pour mixture over fish, and marinate for about 1 hour. Drain and reserve marinade, pat fish dry, and place trout on a grill over charcoal coals. Grill for about 5 minutes on each side, brushing lightly with marinade from time to time.

In a mixing bowl, blend softened butter with chopped parsley, a pinch of salt, fresh ground white pepper, and a bit of lemon juice. Blend with a wooden spoon to a thick creamy texture, and spoon into a sauceboat.

Arrange trout on a serving platter; garnish with parsley sprigs (or watercress) and lemon slices. Accompany with parslied butter for individual service at table.

Lobster in Cream Sauce (p. 65)

Brook Trout Meunière

Yield: 4 servings

4 small brook trout (about ¾ – 1 lb each)
salt
black pepper, freshly ground
all-purpose flour for dredging
6 Tb butter
2 Tb chopped fresh parsley

Clean trout, rinse well in cold running water, and pat dry thoroughly. Cut several diagonal slashes in the sides. Season inside and out with salt and fresh ground pepper, then dredge lightly in flour. Melt 3 tablespoons of butter in a skillet until foaming. Set trout in the pan, and sauté until well browned on both sides.

With a spatula, transfer fish to a serving platter, sprinkle with chopped parsley, and pour pan juices over them. Return skillet to heat; quickly heat remaining 3 tablespoons of butter until nut brown, and pour over fish. Serve piping hot.

Poached Brook Trout

Yield: 4 servings

4 small brook trout (about ¾ – 1 lb each)
salt
1 carrot, chopped coarse
1 small onion, chopped coarse
1 stalk celery, chopped coarse
fresh parsley sprigs
1 bay leaf
juice of 1 lemon
6–8 peppercorns
4 Tb butter
2 Tb chopped fresh parsley
1 lemon, sliced

Clean fish, rinse well in cold running water, and pat dry. Set them in a fish poacher or large saucepan, and add water to cover. Add carrot, onion, celery, several parsley sprigs, bay leaf, lemon juice (reserving about 1 tablespoon for sauce), 3 or 4 bruised peppercorns, and salt to taste. Bring to a boil, reduce heat, and simmer very gently for 8 to 10 minutes, or until fish flake easily.

Drain trout carefully, and transfer to a serving platter. Melt butter in a small saucepan, and heat until foaming. Add chopped parsley, reserved lemon juice, a pinch of salt, and a few crushed peppercorns. Pour sauce over trout, and garnish with lemon slices to serve.

Brook Trout in Spicy Tomato Sauce

Yield: 4 servings

4 small brook trout (about ¾–1 lb each)
2 Tb oil
4 Tb butter
1 small onion, chopped
2 carrots, chopped
1 stalk celery, chopped
3 Tb chopped fresh parsley
1 cup dry white wine
salt and pepper
1 bay leaf
1 heaping Tb capers, chopped
8-oz can peeled tomatoes

Clean trout, rinse well in cold running water, and pat dry. In a large ovenproof skillet or saucepan, heat oil and 2 tablespoons of butter. Add chopped onion, carrots, celery, and parsley, and sauté until carrot is nearly tender. Add trout to the skillet, and pour wine over the fish. Simmer gently until wine evaporates partially, season lightly with salt and pepper, then add bay leaf and chopped capers.

Preheat oven to 400°. Press tomatoes through a food mill or sieve into the pan, and continue simmering gently over low heat until sauce thickens slightly. Move skillet to preheated oven and bake for about 20 minutes, or until fish flakes easily. Transfer trout to a serving platter and keep hot. Strain sauce or press through a food mill into a small saucepot, and add remaining tablespoon of butter in bits. Heat just long enough to melt butter and warm sauce through, taste for seasoning, then pour over trout to serve.

Poached Marinated Salmon Trout

Yield: 4 servings

1 whole salmon trout (about 3–3½ lb)
1½ cups red wine vinegar
1 tsp thyme
1 small carrot, chopped coarse
1 small onion, chopped coarse
1 stalk celery, chopped coarse
1 bay leaf
fresh parsley sprigs
2 Tb lemon juice
peppercorns
salt
1-2 lemons, cut in wedges

Clean fish, rinse well in cold running water, and pat dry. With a sharp knife, cut the spine near the center to keep from curling during cooking. Set fish in a deep dish, and pour vinegar mixed with thyme over it; marinate for at least 30 minutes, turning occasionally.

Fill a fish poacher or large saucepan about halfway with water. Add chopped carrot, onion, and celery, bay leaf, a few parsley sprigs, lemon juice, 4 or 5 bruised peppercorns, and salt to taste. Bring to a boil, lower fish into the pan, and reduce heat. Add several tablespoons of marinade to the water, and simmer gently for 7 or 8 minutes, or just until fish flakes easily.

Drain trout, transfer to a platter, garnish with parsley sprigs and lemon wedges to serve. Accompany fish with a sauceboat of very hot lemon butter for individual service.

Shellfish

Clams Marinara

Yield: 4 servings

4 doz steamer clams
½ cup oil
½ cup dry white wine
3 garlic cloves, chopped
¼ cup chopped fresh parsley
5–6 peppercorns, crushed (or dash of hot pepper flakes)
1-lb can peeled tomatoes, drained and chopped
salt
4 slices toasted bread, cut in triangles

Scrub clams thoroughly in cold running water. Put them in a deep saucepan, add oil and wine, cover tightly, and steam over high heat for a few minutes, or just until all shells are open. Transfer clams to a hot platter, and strain cooking liquid into another saucepan. Add chopped garlic and parsley, crushed peppercorns, and tomatoes. Blend well, adding salt if necessary, then simmer rapidly over high heat to reduce sauce.

Put clams in pan with sauce, stir gently to spread sauce evenly over clams, and pile them on a serving platter. Garnish wih chopped parsley, and accompany individual portions with toast points.

Grilled Lobster Flambé

Yield: 4 servings

2 whole lobsters (about 2–2½ lb each)
salt
4 Tb butter, melted
paprika
½ cup brandy, warmed
2 Tb chopped fresh parsley

Fill a large kettle or pot three-quarters full with lightly salted water, and bring to a rolling boil. Plunge lobsters into the water, and return to a boil, then cover and continue cooking for 5 to 8 minutes, or until lobsters turn pink. Drain lobsters, let stand briefly to cool, and dry thoroughly.

Cut lobsters in half lengthwise, without removing meat from their shells. Brush the cut surfaces generously with melted butter, sprinkle with paprika, and set on a hot grill (or else under a broiler), making sure that no flames touch them directly. Turn every few minutes with a spatula, and cook for about 10 minutes in all for each side, basting occasionally with more melted butter. (Be very careful in turning lobster on a grill; do not use a fork, since the flesh should not be pierced during cooking.) When lobster is tender and golden brown on the open surface, transfer to a metal platter, pour on brandy, flame, and serve immediately. Garnish lightly with chopped parsley, and serve with additional melted butter on the side.

Country-Style Mussels (p. 66)

Spicy Mussels in White Wine (p. 68)

Boiled Lobster

Yield: 4 servings

2 whole lobsters (about 2–2½ lb each)
salt and pepper
2 Tb butter (or oil)
juice of 1 lemon (or ½ cup dry white wine)
fresh parsley sprigs

Use a pot large enough to hold lobsters with enough water to cover. Fill pot with water to about three-quarters capacity; add 1 tablespoon of salt per quart of water and a generous sprinkling of pepper. Add butter, lemon juice, and several parsley sprigs, and bring to a rolling boil. Plunge lobsters into water, return to a boil, and time the cooking from this point on. Cover pot, and continue cooking at a slower boil. Allow 12 to 15 minutes of cooking time for a 2-pound lobster, and about 3 minutes more for each additional pound of lobster. (Lobsters will turn bright pink when properly cooked.)

Lobster Catalan

Yield: 4 servings

2 whole lobsters (about 2–2½ lb each)
salt
1 carrot, chopped
1 stalk celery, chopped
1 large onion, chopped
2 bay leaves
fresh parsley sprigs
juice of ½ lemon
8 peppercorns
2 garlic cloves, minced
6–8 almonds, chopped fine
3 Tb chopped fresh parsley
3 Tb oil
thyme
¼ cup brandy (or dry sherry)
black pepper, freshly ground
1 Tb unsweetened cocoa (optional)
saffron

Fill a large kettle or pot three-quarters full with lightly salted water. Add carrot, celery, half the chopped onion, 1 bay leaf, several sprigs of parsley, lemon juice, and 5 peppercorns. Bring to a boil, and continue boiling for about 10 minutes. Plunge lobsters in the rapidly boiling water, and again bring to a boil. Begin timing from this point (i.e., when water returns to boiling). Cover the pot, and boil lobster for 12 to 15 minutes. Drain, reserving ¼ cup of cooking liquid, remove meat from lobsters, and cut in bite-size pieces.

In a mortar or a sturdy small bowl, combine garlic, almonds, chopped parsley, and remaining 3 peppercorns, then mash them together. Sauté remaining half of chopped onion in oil. Add a pinch of thyme and 1 crushed bay leaf. Stir to blend, and add lobster meat, salt and fresh ground pepper, and sauté briefly. Stir in brandy, and simmer until it evaporates. Dissolve cocoa and a pinch of saffron in reserved ¼ cup of cooking liquid. Add mashed ingredients to the pan, along with cocoa and saffron, and continue cooking over low heat for about 30 minutes. Serve piping hot, over a bed of cooked white rice.

Lobster with Brandy Sauce

Yield: 4 servings

2 whole lobsters (about 2–2½ lb each)
¼ lb butter
½ cup brandy (or dry sherry)
salt
cayenne pepper
juice of ½ lemon

First cook lobsters according to instructions in recipe for Boiled Lobster (see Index). Then, with a sharp knife, make a vertical cut down through the lower part of the shell, and extract tail meat in a single piece. Crack claws and antennae with a nutcracker and extract meat.

Brown butter in a skillet. Slice tail meat about ½ inch thick, and chop remaining meat coarse. Sauté lobster meat in brown butter, pour on brandy, sprinkle lightly with salt, and simmer over low heat until brandy evaporates. Simmer a few minutes longer, then transfer lobster meat to a hot serving platter. Season lightly with cayenne pepper and lemon juice, then bring pan juices just to the boiling point, and pour over lobster to serve.

Lobster in Cream Sauce

Yield: 4 servings

2 whole lobsters (about 2–2½ lb each)
8 Tb butter
salt
½ cup brandy (or dry sherry)
1 cup heavy cream
cayenne pepper

First cook lobsters according to instructions in recipe for Boiled Lobster (see Index). Rinse cooked lobsters, drain well, and cut off legs and antennae. Make a deep slit along the tail, and extract tail meat. Slice tail meat in segments, and discard the tip. Split head, and discard head sac; crack claw, leg, and antennae shells. Extract meat from head, claws, legs, and antennae.

Sauté lobster meat in 4 tablespoons of butter until golden brown; sprinkle lightly with salt, and cook for a few minutes longer. Pour brandy over lobster meat, then simmer until liquor is reduced by half, and add heavy cream. Taste for seasoning, and add salt if necessary. Season to taste with cayenne pepper, then simmer gently for about 20 minutes.

With a slotted spoon, transfer lobster meat to a deep serving platter, and keep hot. Blend remaining 4 tablespoons of butter, a bit at a time, with cooking juices in the pan. Bring to a boil, pour sauce over lobster meat, and serve immediately.

Mussels Marinara

Yield: 4 servings

4 doz mussels
1 cup olive oil
1 garlic clove, chopped
2 Tb chopped fresh parsley
salt
black pepper, freshly ground
1 cup dry white wine
8 slices crusty bread, toasted

Clean mussels with a stiff brush, pull off "beard," and rinse mussels thoroughly in cold running water. Soak in cold water to cover for about 1 hour, and discard any mussels that float to the top. Heat ½ cup olive oil in a large deep saucepan. Combine garlic and parsley, and sauté half the mixture. Add mussels to the pan, cover, and steam for about 5 minutes, or just until shells open. Season with salt and fresh ground pepper, then gradually pour in dry wine. Simmer gently for about 5 minutes. Combine remaining oil and reserved garlic-parsley mixture, and spread on toasted bread. Serve mussels and cooking liquid in soup bowls atop slices of seasoned bread.

Mussels Oreganata

Yield: 4 servings

3 doz mussels
about 5 Tb oil
dry white wine
8-oz can peeled tomatoes
⅓ cup bread crumbs
1 Tb chopped fresh parsley
oregano
2 Tb butter, melted

Clean and soak mussels as in recipe for Mussels Marinara above. Steam mussels open by sautéeing in a large, tightly covered saucepan with 3 tablespoons of oil and a few tablespoons of dry wine. Remove opened mussels from the pan; reserve broth.

Preheat oven to 350°. Drain tomatoes, and press through a sieve or food mill. Combine with bread crumbs, chopped parsley, a generous pinch of oregano, melted butter, and a bit of cooking broth from the mussels. Set out steamed mussels on the half shell on a large cookie sheet (or in a large shallow baking dish), and sprinkle bread crumb mixture generously over them. Dribble on a little more oil, and bake in preheated oven for 10 to 15 minutes, or until bread crumbs become slightly dry and crusty.

Country-Style Mussels

Yield: 4 servings

4 doz mussels
4 slices bacon
4 Tb butter, melted
tomato sauce (preferably homemade)

Clean and soak mussels as in recipe for Mussels Marinara above. Pry open and extract mussels; discard shells and pat mussels dry.

Preheat oven to 425°. Spear mussels on 4 skewers, and spiral a slice of bacon around each. Butter a baking dish, and arrange skewers in it. Baste with melted butter, and bake in preheated oven for 5 to 10 minutes, or until bacon is nicely browned. Accompany with warmed tomato sauce in a sauceboat for individual service at table.

Oysters and Caviar (p. 68)

French-Style Mussels

Yield: 4 servings

3 doz mussels
2 Tb chopped scallions
¼ cup chopped fresh parsley
black pepper, freshly ground
thyme
1 bay leaf
2 cups dry white wine
1 Tb butter
1 Tb all-purpose flour
salt
juice of ½ lemon

Clean and soak mussels as in recipe for Mussels Marinara (see Index). Put mussels in a large saucepan, add 1 tablespoon of chopped scallions, 2 tablespoons of chopped parsley, a pinch of pepper and thyme, bay leaf, and 1 cup of dry wine. Bring quickly to a boil, cover, lower heat, and steam for about 5 minutes, or just until shells open. Remove mussels to a large bowl, and keep warm. Strain cooking liquid through a cheesecloth or a fine sieve, and reserve.

Put remaining cup of wine and 1 tablespoon of scallions in a saucepan, and simmer until wine is reduced by half, then add reserved cooking liquid. Cream together the butter and flour until smooth, and blend mixture into sauce. Add salt to taste and lemon juice.

Discard upper half of each mussel shell, and arrange mussels on the half shell on a serving platter. Pour sauce over mussels, sprinkle with remaining chopped parsley, and serve piping hot.

Spicy Mussels in White Wine

Yield: 4 servings

4 doz mussels
⅓ cup oil
3 garlic cloves, sliced
hot pepper flakes
½ cup dry white wine
½ cup chopped fresh parsley

Clean and soak mussels as in recipe for Mussels Marinara (see Index). Heat oil in a large saucepan, and sauté garlic and a sprinkling of hot pepper flakes. Add mussels, wine, and 3 tablespoons of water. Cover tightly, and steam for about 5 minutes, or just until shells open. Pile mussels in a deep bowl. Strain cooking liquids through cheesecloth or a fine sieve, and pour over mussels. Sprinkle with chopped parsley, and serve immediately accompanied with crusty French or Italian bread.

Oysters and Caviar

Yield: 4 servings

2 or 3 doz oysters
black caviar
2–3 lemons, sliced
buttered bread

Shuck oysters, reserve half the shells, and pat oysters dry. Scrub the shells, and rinse thoroughly in cold water. Place about 1 tablespoon of caviar in each half shell, set oysters on caviar, and garnish serving plate with lemon slices. Serve with thin slices of buttered bread.

Oysters with Champagne Sauce

Yield: 4 servings

about 2 doz oysters, depending on size
2 cups champagne (or other dry sparkling wine)
½ cup heavy cream
2 egg yolks
salt
black pepper, freshly ground

Shuck oysters, reserve half the shells, and place oysters and their liquid in a saucepan. Add champagne, and simmer gently for 3 minutes. Remove from heat, drain oysters, and reserve cooking liquid. Scrub shells, rinse thoroughly in cold water, and dry.

Preheat oven to 450°. Reheat the cooking liquid, beat heavy cream into egg yolks, and blend mixture into warm cooking liquid. Stirring constantly, reduce sauce slightly over low heat. Remove from heat, and season to taste with salt and fresh ground pepper.

Arrange half shells in a baking dish, place an oyster in each, and pour sauce over them. Bake in preheated oven for only a minute or two, and serve immediately. A dark coarse bread, such as pumpernickel, is a good accompaniment.

Barbecued Jumbo Shrimp

Yield: 4 to 6 servings

2 doz jumbo shrimp
salt
paprika
2 lemons, cut in half
fresh parsley sprigs

Rinse and dry shrimp thoroughly. Spear equally on 4 stainless steel skewers, and grill over charcoal (or else under a broiler), turning occasionally, until an even golden brown. Transfer shrimp to a serving platter, sprinkle lightly with salt and paprika, and garnish with lemon halves and parsley sprigs.

Brandied Shrimp Cocktail

Yield: 4 servings

2 doz large shrimp, peeled and deveined
salt and pepper
top leaves from several celery stalks
1 cup mayonnaise
¼ cup brandy (or dry sherry)
2 Tb catsup
½ Tb Worcestershire sauce
1 stalk celery, chopped
lettuce leaves

To a large saucepan of rapidly boiling water add about 1 teaspoon of salt, ½ teaspoon of pepper, and celery leaves, and boil for 10 minutes. Add shrimp, return water to a boil, lower heat, and simmer for about 5 minutes, or just until shrimp turns pink. Drain and let stand to cool. Slice shrimp in half lengthwise, and reserve.

Combine mayonnaise, brandy, catsup, and Worcestershire sauce, blending well. Divide sauce in 3 equal portions. Add chopped celery to one, and sliced shrimp to another. Line 4 seafood cocktail cups with fresh lettuce leaves. Layer first with celery sauce, then the shrimp sauce. Top with remaining sauce, and chill for at least 30 minutes before serving.

Curried Shrimp

Yield: 4 servings

2 lb small shrimp, peeled and deveined
3 Tb butter
¼ lb fresh mushrooms, sliced or chopped coarse
salt
2–3 Tb dry white wine
1½ cups Curry Sauce (see Index)
1 small truffle (optional)

Preheat oven to 400°. Rinse and dry shrimp thoroughly. Heat butter in a skillet, add shrimp, mushrooms, and salt to taste, then sauté over medium heat until shrimp are lightly browned. Pour a little dry wine into the pan, and simmer until wine evaporates. Add half the curry sauce, mix well, and remove from heat. Divide mixture into 4 individual casseroles (or very large seashells), cover with remaining sauce, and bake for a few minutes, or just until hot and bubbly. Garnish with thin slices of truffle just before serving.

Shrimp Croquettes

Yield: 4 servings

1½ lb shrimp, peeled and deveined
1 cup dry white wine
1 small onion, chopped
1 small carrot, chopped
1 stalk celery, chopped
1 bay leaf
salt
4 peppercorns
2 Tb chopped fresh parsley
4 Tb butter
¼ cup all-purpose flour
1 cup milk, heated
black pepper, freshly ground
nutmeg, freshly grated
1 egg yolk
½ cup grated Gruyère cheese
2 eggs, lightly beaten
fine bread crumbs for dredging
oil for deep frying

Rinse shrimp well, and place in a saucepan with water to cover. Add dry wine, chopped onion, carrot, and celery, bay leaf, bruised peppercorns, and salt to taste. Bring to a boil, lower heat, and simmer shrimp for 3 to 5 minutes, or until just pink. Strain cooking liquid into a clean saucepan, reserving vegetable residue. Bring cooking liquid to a boil again, and simmer rapidly until liquid is reduced to just a few tablespoons. Chop cooked shrimp fine. Squeeze excess water from cooked vegetables, chop lightly, and mix with chopped parsley.

Melt butter over medium heat, add flour, and cook, stirring constantly until well blended. Pour hot milk into flour mixture, still stirring constantly, and cook until thickened and smooth. Season to taste with salt, pepper, and nutmeg. Remove from heat, and blend in egg yolk, then grated Gruyère, and finally chopped shrimp, a bit of the vegetable mix, and the reduced cooking liquid. Let stand to cool.

With moistened hands, form egg-shaped croquettes. Dip croquettes in beaten egg, then in bread crumbs. Deep-fry in very hot oil, preheated to 375°. When golden brown, drain on paper towels before serving. Batter-fried zucchini sticks would be suitable accompaniment for croquettes.

Shrimp Croquettes (p. 70) and Fried Marinated Sardines (p. 38)

Shrimp Fritters

Yield: 4 servings

20 jumbo shrimp, peeled and deveined
salt
black pepper, freshly ground
juice of 1 lemon
2 eggs
⅔ cup all-purpose flour
2–3 Tb brandy (or dry sherry)
1 Tb olive oil
oil for deep frying
2 lemons, quartered

Rinse shrimp, dry thoroughly, and place in a mixing bowl. Season lightly with salt and fresh ground black pepper, stir in lemon juice, and marinate for about 30 minutes, stirring occasionally. Beat eggs in a mixing bowl; gradually add flour, and blend well until smooth. Add a tablespoonful of brandy, olive oil, a pinch of salt and pepper, and enough lukewarm water to make a fairly thin batter. Drain marinade from shrimp, then put shrimp in batter and coat well.

Preheat oil in a deep-fryer to 370° and, using a spoon to transfer each shrimp and a little batter to the oil, fry a few at a time until golden brown. Remove fried shrimp with a slotted spoon, and drain on paper towels. Serve piping hot, garnished with lemon wedges.

Shrimp with Mustard Sauce

Yield: 4 servings

2 lb small shrimp, peeled and deveined
salt
2 Tb oil
2 Tb butter
1 small onion, chopped
1 Tb tomato purée (or catsup)
1 Tb prepared mustard
juice of ½ lemon
1 cup dry white wine

Rinse shrimp well, and sprinkle lightly with salt. Heat oil and butter, and sauté onion until transparent. Add shrimp, and brown lightly. Stir in tomato purée, mustard, and lemon juice, blending well. Add dry wine, mix well, and simmer gently for about 10 minutes. Shrimp may be served hot, over a bed of cooked white rice, or as a chilled appetizer or salad accompaniment.

Shrimp and Rice au Gratin

Yield: 4 servings

1 lb small shrimp
½ lb long-grain rice
salt
about 2 cups Béchamel Sauce (see Index)
½ cup grated Parmesan cheese
1 cup heavy cream (or half-and-half)
white pepper
¼ lb fontina cheese, sliced thin

Cook rice in lightly salted boiling water to cover, drain, and place in a heatproof dish lined with a clean kitchen towel. Cover with towel, and place in a low oven for 10 to 15 minutes to dry thoroughly.

Combine Béchamel sauce, grated Parmesan, heavy cream, and a pinch of pepper.

Cook shrimp in lightly salted boiling water until just tender, about 5 to 8 minutes. Let cool slightly, peel, and devein. Add shrimp and half the sauce to cooked rice in a mixing bowl.

Preheat oven to 350°. Butter an ovenproof casserole, and fill with rice mixture. Spread fontina slices evenly on top, pour remaining sauce over all, and bake for about 10 minutes, or until heated through and golden brown on top.

Sautéed Soft-Shell Crabs

Yield: 4 servings

8–12 soft-shell crabs
fine dry bread crumbs for dredging
salt and pepper
½ cup butter
juice of ½ lemon
2 Tb minced parsley

With a sharp knife, remove the "apron," or flap, that folds beneath the rear of the underside of the crabs. Turn crab over and cut off face, starting just back of the eyes. Pull back each point, then pull off all the spongy material that is exposed. Rinse and dry crabs thoroughly.

Combine bread crumbs, salt, and pepper, and dredge crabs in the mixture. Heat butter in a large skillet until foaming, add crabs, and sauté quickly until golden brown on both sides. Remove cooked crabs to a heated platter, add lemon juice and parsley to the pan, and stir with a wooden spoon to blend with cooking juices. Pour sauce over crabs, and serve immediately.

Deep-Fried Squid

Yield: 4 servings

2 lb baby squid, cleaned and sliced in ½-inch
  rings*
salt
all-purpose flour for dredging
2 eggs, lightly beaten
fine bread crumbs for dredging
oil for deep frying
2 lemons, quartered

Rinse squid well, and pat dry. Sprinkle with salt, and dredge lightly in flour; then dip in beaten egg, and dredge in bread crumbs, coating them evenly. Deep-fry in very hot oil preheated to 375°. Remove with a slotted spoon, and drain on paper towels before serving, garnished with lemon wedges.

* For instructions on cleaning squid, see recipe for Stuffed Squid (see Index).

Spicy Squid Vinaigrette

Yield: 4 servings

2 lb baby squid, cleaned and sliced in ½-inch
　rings*
6 Tb oil
salt
hot pepper flakes
1 small onion, minced
2 Tb wine vinegar
2 Tb chopped fresh parsley

Heat 3 tablespoons of oil in a skillet, and sauté squid for 4 or 5 minutes, or just until golden in color. Combine salt and hot pepper flakes to taste with minced onion, 3 tablespoons of oil, and vinegar, blending well. Add squid, and stir to coat thoroughly. Chill until ready to serve, then garnish with chopped parsley.

　* For instructions on cleaning squid, see recipe for Stuffed Squid below.

Stuffed Squid

Yield: 4 servings

2 lb baby squid
1 garlic clove
¼ cup fresh parsley leaves, loosely packed
⅓ cup fresh bread crumbs
oil
salt and pepper
⅓ cup dry white wine

To clean squid: Remove ink sac, mouth, eyes, and internal cartilage (cuttlebone). Peel off outer skin, rinse in several changes of cold water, and remove sacs from tentacles.

Cut off and mince tentacles together with garlic and parsley. (This may be done, in a food processor, taking care to mince rather than purée the ingredients). Transfer to a mixing bowl, add bread crumbs, 3 tablespoons of oil, and salt and pepper to taste, blending well. Stuff squid bodies with this mixture. Sew openings with string, or close them with toothpicks.

Preheat oven to 375°. Oil a baking dish large enough to hold squid in a single layer, and set stuffed squid in it. Dribble on a little more oil, add dry wine, and sprinkle lightly with salt and pepper. Bake in preheated oven for about 45 minutes, transfer to a heated platter, and serve immediately.

Shrimp and Rice au Gratin (p. 73)

Fish Soups and Stews

Bouillabaisse

Yield: 4 servings

2 lb assorted firm-fleshed fish (fish steaks and
  fillets)
1 lb medium-size shrimp
1 doz mussels
½ cup oil
1 onion, chopped
1 garlic clove, chopped
hot pepper flakes
1-lb can peeled tomatoes
¼ cup chopped fresh parsley
1 tsp celery seed
1½ cups dry white wine
salt
8 slices day-old crusty bread
1 garlic clove, split
black pepper, freshly ground

Rinse fish well in cold running water, and cut in large chunks. Heat oil (in a large earthenware casserole with a cover, if possible), and sauté onion, garlic, mussels, and a dash of hot pepper flakes in covered casserole or saucepan until mussels are all open and onion is transparent. Press tomatoes through a food mill or sieve, and add to the pan with chopped parsley, celery seed, dry wine, salt to taste, and about 3 cups of water. Bring to a boil, lower heat, and simmer gently for about 20 minutes. Remove mussels and reserve.

Add the fish chunks—beginning with the firmer-fleshed ones which take longer to cook (allowing only a few minutes for the shrimp)—and stir well; simmer gently for about 20 minutes longer. Rub stale bread with cut faces of garlic, and set 2 slices in each of 4 shallow soup bowls. Ladle fish chunks, shrimp, mussels, and soup over them, sprinkle generously with fresh ground pepper, and garnish with a bit of chopped parsley.

Oyster Stew

Yield: 4 servings

2 doz oysters
¼ cup butter
Worcestershire sauce
celery salt
paprika
2 cups clam broth
4 cups milk (or half-and-half)
white pepper, preferably freshly ground

Open oysters, and reserve their liquor. In a saucepan, melt butter and add a generous pinch of Worcestershire sauce, celery salt, and paprika. Stir in oysters and their liquor, together with the clam broth, and bring to a simmer over medium heat. Cook just until the edges of oysters begin curling slightly. Add milk, bring just to the boiling point, and remove from heat immediately. Serve in a tureen or in individual soup bowls, garnished with a sprinkling of paprika or a pinch of minced fresh parsley.

Adriatic Fish Soup

Yield: 4 servings

2 lb assorted fish (e.g., mullet, porgy, sole,
  whiting)
¾ lb squid
1 large onion, chopped
1 garlic clove, chopped
½ cup olive oil
saffron
1 cup dry white wine
clam broth (or fish or vegetable stock)
4 thick slices day-old crusty bread, toasted
2 Tb chopped fresh parsley

Clean fish, rinse well in cold running water, and cut in large chunks. Clean squid, and rinse well; remove skin and membrane. Cut squid in ¼-inch rings. Tentacles may be used whole or cut in bite-size pieces. Pat fish and squid dry with paper towels.

Heat oil (in a large earthenware casserole, if possible), and sauté onion and garlic until onion is transparent. Dissolve saffron in 2 tablespoons of water, and add. Season to taste with salt and pepper, stirring well.

Add fish slices and squid to the pan, and stir gently to coat. Pour in white wine and enough broth (or water) to cover. Bring to a boil, lower heat, and simmer gently for 15 to 20 minutes, or until squid is tender. (Do not overcook.) Taste soup for seasoning, and adjust if necessary.

To serve, set a slice of toast in each of 4 soup plates, and sprinkle with ½ tablespoon of parsley; ladle fish and broth into the plates, and serve piping hot.

Sardinian Fish Stew (Zuppa di Pesce)

Yield: 4 servings

2½ lb assorted firm-fleshed, moderately fatty fish
  (e.g., mackerel, mullet, porgy), including some
  squid and eel
salt
oil
1 onion, chopped
hot pepper flakes
1-lb can peeled tomatoes
⅓ cup dry white wine
1 tsp celery seed (or fennel seed)
½ tsp thyme
1 garlic clove, split
8 slices day-old crusty bread
2 Tb chopped fresh parsley
black pepper, freshly ground

Clean fish, rinse well in cold running water, then poach each kind separately in lightly salted water to cover, until barely tender. Drain fish, and reserve poaching liquid from each. Cut fish in large chunks. Slice eel in ½-inch rounds, and squid in ¼-inch rings. Heat oil (in a large earthenware casserole, if possible), and sauté onion and hot pepper flakes; then sauté eel and squid briefly, just till light golden. Put poached fish chunks in casserole; stir gently to coat.

Press tomatoes through a food mill or sieve, then add to casserole, cook for 2 or 3 minutes, and pour in wine and enough of poaching liquid to cover. Stir in celery seed and thyme, and simmer gently for about 5 to 10 minutes. Taste for seasoning, and add salt if necessary.

To serve, rub cut faces of garlic over bread slices, toast lightly, and set 2 slices in each of 4 shallow soup bowls. Spoon fish chunks onto bread, pour on broth, and serve piping hot, with a light garnish of chopped parsley and a sprinkling of fresh ground pepper.

Seafood Gumbo

Yield: 4 servings

1½ doz oysters
1 lb small shrimp, peeled and deveined
1 cup cooked crab meat (optional)
2 Tb oil
1 large onion, chopped
1 garlic clove, chopped
1 stalk celery, chopped
1 sweet green pepper, chopped
2 Tb all-purpose flour
2 Tb minced fresh parsley
thyme
2 bay leaves
salt and pepper
cayenne pepper
1 cup clam broth
½–1 tsp gumbo filé powder* (optional)
about 3 cups cooked rice

Open oysters, and reserve their liquor. In a deep heavy saucepan, heat oil and sauté chopped onion, garlic, celery, and green pepper. Sprinkle the mixture with flour and stir until lightly browned, then add parsley, a pinch of thyme, and bay leaves, blending well. Season to taste with salt, pepper, and cayenne, and stir in reserved oyster liquor, clam broth, and 4 cups of water. Bring to a boil, reduce heat, and simmer gently for 1½ hours. Add shrimp, and simmer gently for another 20 minutes. Stir in crab meat and oysters, and simmer just until the edges of oysters begin curling. Remove saucepan from heat, and stir in filé powder. Serve piping hot in deep soup bowls, with a mound of cooked rice at one side.

* Gumbo filé powder can be found in gourmet sections of supermarkets and in specialty food shops. It is added to the dish only after the cooking is complete, and should not be reheated.

Yugoslavian Fish Soup

Yield: 4 servings

2 lb assorted firm-fleshed fish (e.g. cod, halibut, mullet, sea trout, tilefish)
½ cup oil
1 large onion, chopped
1-lb can peeled tomatoes, chopped
1 Tb tomato paste
1 cup dry rosé wine
2–3 Tb wine vinegar
clam broth (or fish or vegetable stock)
1 Tb paprika
salt and pepper
¼ cup chopped fresh parsley

Clean fish, rinse well in cold running water, and cut in 1-inch slices. Heat oil (in a large earthenware casserole, if possible), and sauté onion until transparent. Stir in fish chunks, and sauté until they are slightly golden. Add tomatoes and tomato paste, stirring gently to blend. Pour in wine, vinegar, and if necessary, just enough broth (or water) to cover. Stir in paprika and salt and pepper to taste, then bring to a boil. Lower heat, and simmer gently for about 20 minutes, or until fish flakes easily, stirring occasionally. Sprinkle with chopped parsley before serving, and accompany with cooked white rice.

Index of Recipes by Category